SIGN OF
CAFE AND RESTAURANT

DESIGN MEDIA PUBLISHING (UK) LIMITED

SIGN OF
CAFE AND RESTAURANT

Coffee & Kitchen

WWW.COFFEEANDKITCHEN.AT

ÖFFNUNGSZEITEN

MO–FR 07:00–19:30 UHR

WLAN

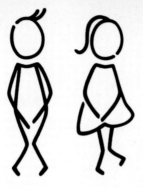

KEINE SCHLECHTE LAUNE
NO BAD TEMPER

**KRAWATTE? PROBIER'S
MAL OHNE**
TIE? WHY NOT TRY
WITHOUT

KEINE BETRIEBSSPIONAGE
NO SPIES

007

Our eggs are **fresh**: gathered by hand from straw-filled nests.

Our frozen custard is made with **five ingredients**: milk, cream, egg, sugar and vanilla.

All of our meats have no hormones, steroids or any other genetically altered process.

We are **locally owned** and operated.

Our smoothies are made with **100% fruit**.

DRAMA
BURGER

THE LADI
HAPPY VALLE

WEDNESDAY, FEBR

HOTSPUR

The Unique Prize
PONY ENTRANCE FEE $5

013

ocio

PDX   ORE

COOPERS·HALL

WINERY AND TAPROOM

4PM — 10PM
SUNDAY — THURSDAY

4PM — 12AM

019

MILLER'S GUILD

SEATTLE, WASHINGTON

DAILY
8 AM to 11 PM

ATRACTIVO

APERITIVO

025

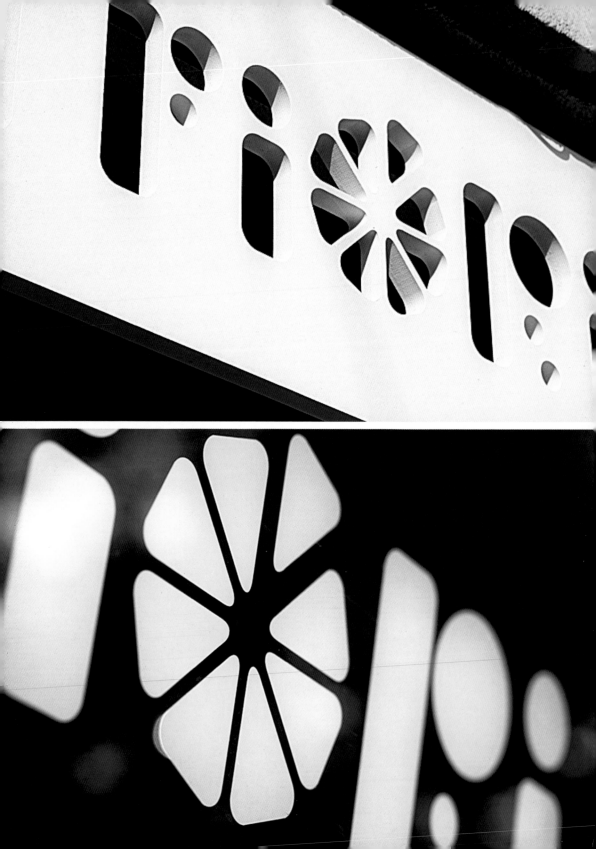

A

LUNES - SÁBADO

9am - 10pm

PANADERÍA
DELIRIO

Baguette Tradicional	Croissant
Campesino Rústico	Chocolatín
Campesino con Aceitunas	Cartera con Crema Pastelera
Integral & Ciabatta	Rol de Pasas con Nueces

Nuestro pan sale del horno a las 9am y a la 1.30pm

$22
$28
$32
$40
$12

Chai latte
Assam (té negro)
Sencha (té verde) $35
Marroquí $30
(té verde con menta) $30

Chocolate caliente $30

Té o café frío

INFUSIONES
Rooibos
Manzanilla bugambilia
Manzana Turca $30
Guayaba $30
Jamaica, jengibre & canela $30
                                 $30
                                 +$5

LASSIES
Platano/cardamomo
Mango/cardamomo $30
Cardamomo $30
Salado $25
                     $25

Agua del dia
Cerveza & Vino $15
                     (12-5pm)

TOASTS
(desayunos)
Jamón & queso con salvia $45
Mozarella, jitomate & hierbas frescas
Tocino, chihuahua & jitomate $45
Tocino, huevo & mayonesa $45

QUESOS

Semiduro de Oveja, Gruyère,
Mozarella Fresco, Gorgonzola,
Ramonetti Doble Crema,
Chihuahua, Real del Castillo,
Brie & Camembert

Selección de pequeños productores,
en su mayoría nacionales.

SÁNDWICHES

Jamón de Pierna & Queso Chihuahua / $60
Pechuga de Pavo, Salame & Queso Gruyère / $65
Prosciutto, Jitomate, Pesto & Arúgula / $65
Queso Brie, Compota de Manzana & Nueces / $65
Croissant con Jamón & Queso / $35
SÁNDWICH DEL DÍA

Preparados diariamente con pan hecho en nuestro horno.

JAMONES, PATES & TERRINAS

Prosciutto, Jamón de Pierna
Pechuga de Pavo & Salami

Campiña, Campiña con Pistache, Legumbres
Cabeza al Perejil & Pato con Avellana

ABARROTES

sal de mar de Cuyutlán
y especias de todo el
mundo. Todos nuestros
productos son hechos
con dedicación :
usando sólo la mejor

Costa Nueva

MARISCOS
Y BAR

Costa Nueva

DE COSTA A COSTA

A FRANCESINHA
QUE SE COME À MÃO

SANDINHA TRADICIONAL
A RECEITA DA FRANCESINHA
TRADICIONAL COM CARNE ASSADA
THE TRADITIONAL WITH ROASTED MEAT

SANDINHA DA HORTA
TOMATE, CEBOLA, COGUMELOS E PASSOS
TOMATO, ONION, MUSHROOMS

A ORIGINAL · DESDE 2014

Sandinha

A FRANCESINHA QUE SE COME À MÃO

037

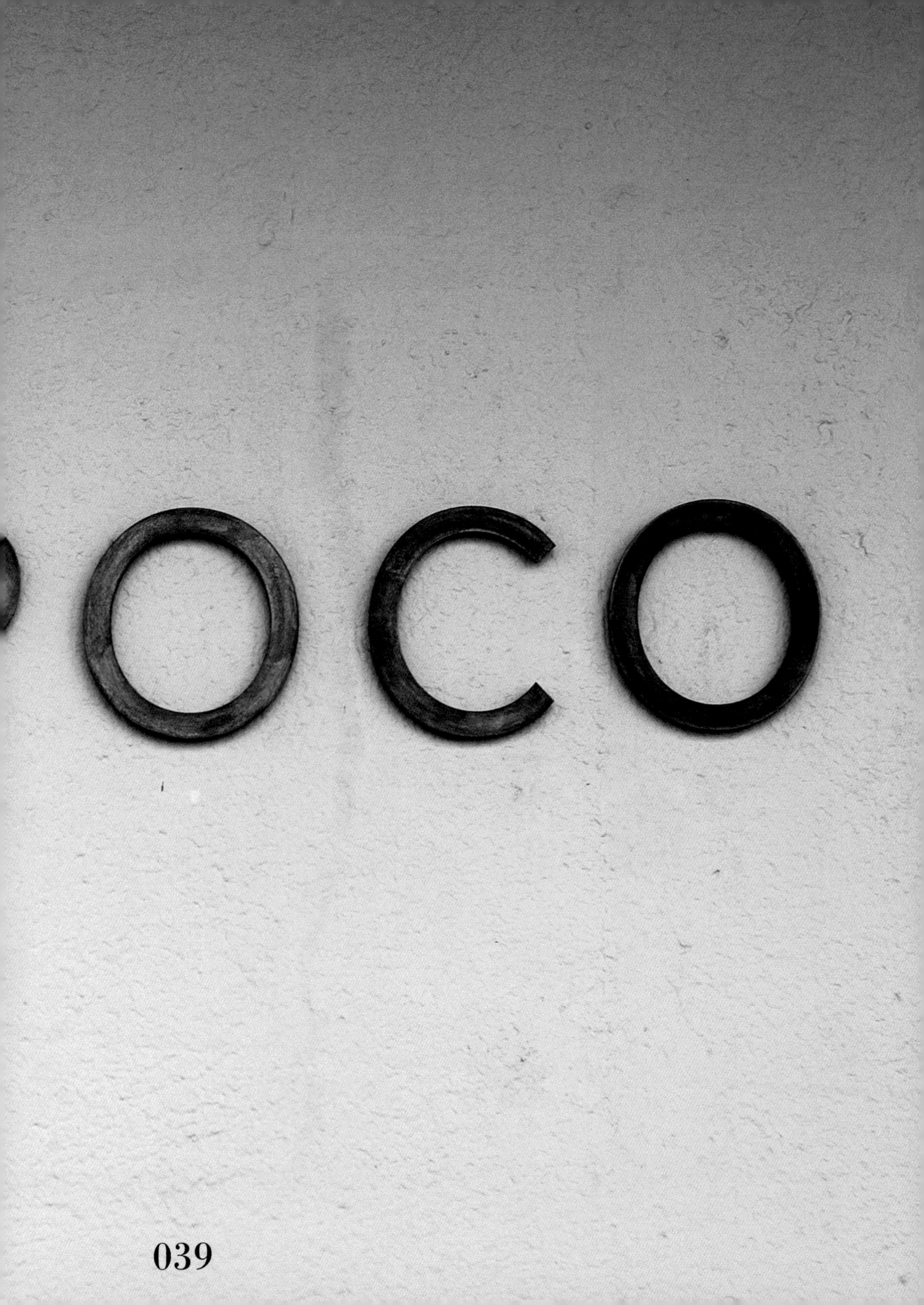
OCO

TACO ANATOMY

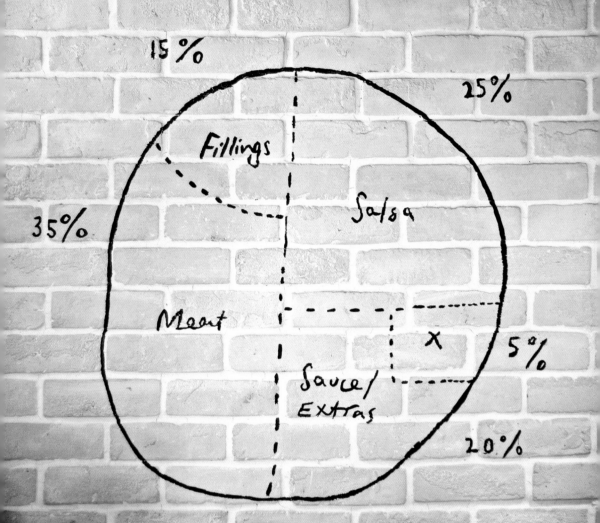

15%

25%

Fillings

Salsa

35%

Meat

X

5%

Sauce/
Extras

20%

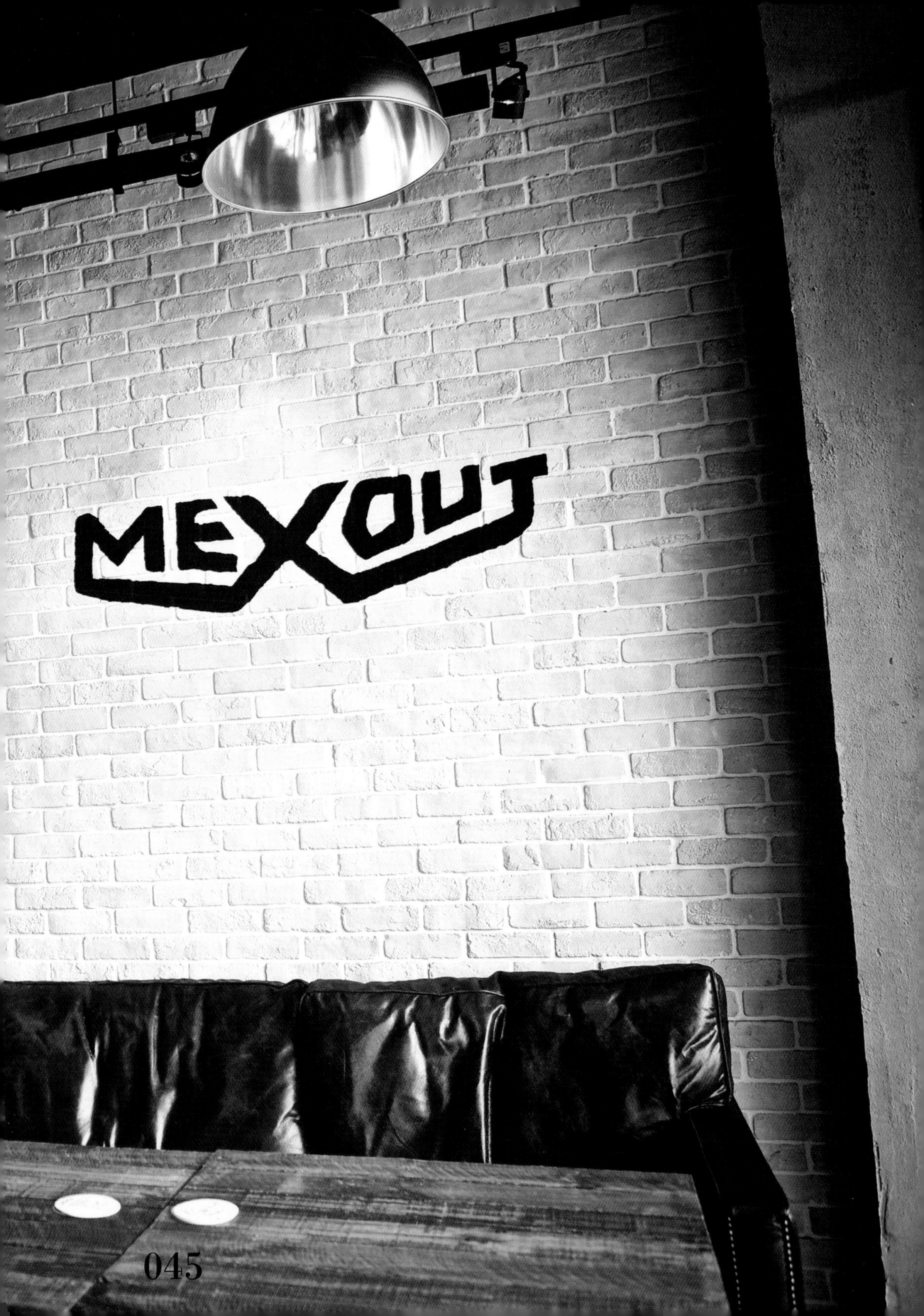
MEXOUT

STYLE

PROTEINS ➤

CHAR-GRILLED CHICKEN
Tex-Mex dry rub with lemon, paprika and black pepper.

COCHINTA PIBIL Pork shoulder braised in orange juice, spices and banana leaf

CHAR-GRILLED CARNE ASADA
Tender marinated air-flown NZ Flank steak in cilantro, onions and paprika
(add $2)

BEEF BARBACOA Beef Brisket dry roasted with cumin, chili powder, beer and dry chilis (add $2)

LAMB BIRRIA Lamb shoulder braised in a blend of spices, onions, and fresh oregano (add $2)

VEGETABLE DE LA CRUZ Capsicum, onions & garlic stewed in a spicy tomato sauce. Will make any carnivore turn VEGETARIAN.

THE TACO CANNON

FILLINGS ➤

MEXICAN STYLE RED RICE Long grain rice lightly mixed with tomato, coriander and lime.

BLACK BEANS Frijoles slowed cooked with soffrito the authentic way VEGETARIAN

PINTO BEANS Slow cooked with parsley, oregano and spices VEGETARIAN

SHREDDED ICEBERG LETTUCE

SOUR CREAM

SALSAS ➤

SALSA FRESCA
Tomato, cilantro, red onion, Jalapeno

SALSA VERDE Tomatillos, cilantro, lime, jalapeno, serrano chiles

SALSA PICANTE Dry chili, roasted onion, roasted tomato, lime, green onions

FIRE ROASTED SALSA
Jalapeno, red onion, capsicum, green onion, cilantro, tomato all roasted over open fire

MANGO PINEAPPLE SALSA Mango, pineapple, red chili, red onion, cilantro, lime

EXTRAS

GUACAMOLE
Our famous take on the goodness of avocado.
(add $2 for any dish)

SHREDDED TASTY CHEESE (add 50¢ for any dish)

MEXOUT

SIDES

CHIPS & SALSA

CHIPS & GUAC

GUACAMOLE TUB

CHURROS & CHOCO SAUCE $5

SOFT DRINKS

VITAMIN WAT

CORONA $9

MARGAR

HAPPY HO

$7 Corona

047

SensacionS
catering

SensacionS
catering

Col.lectivitats

Menjars
per emportar

051

053

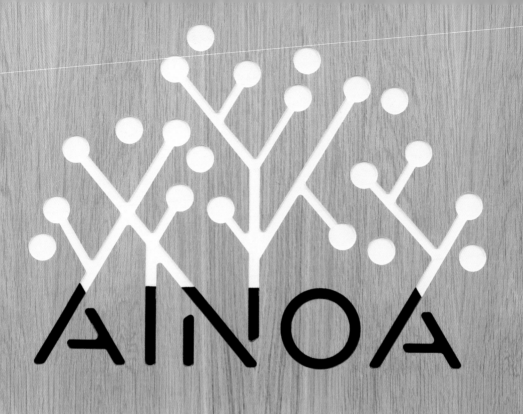

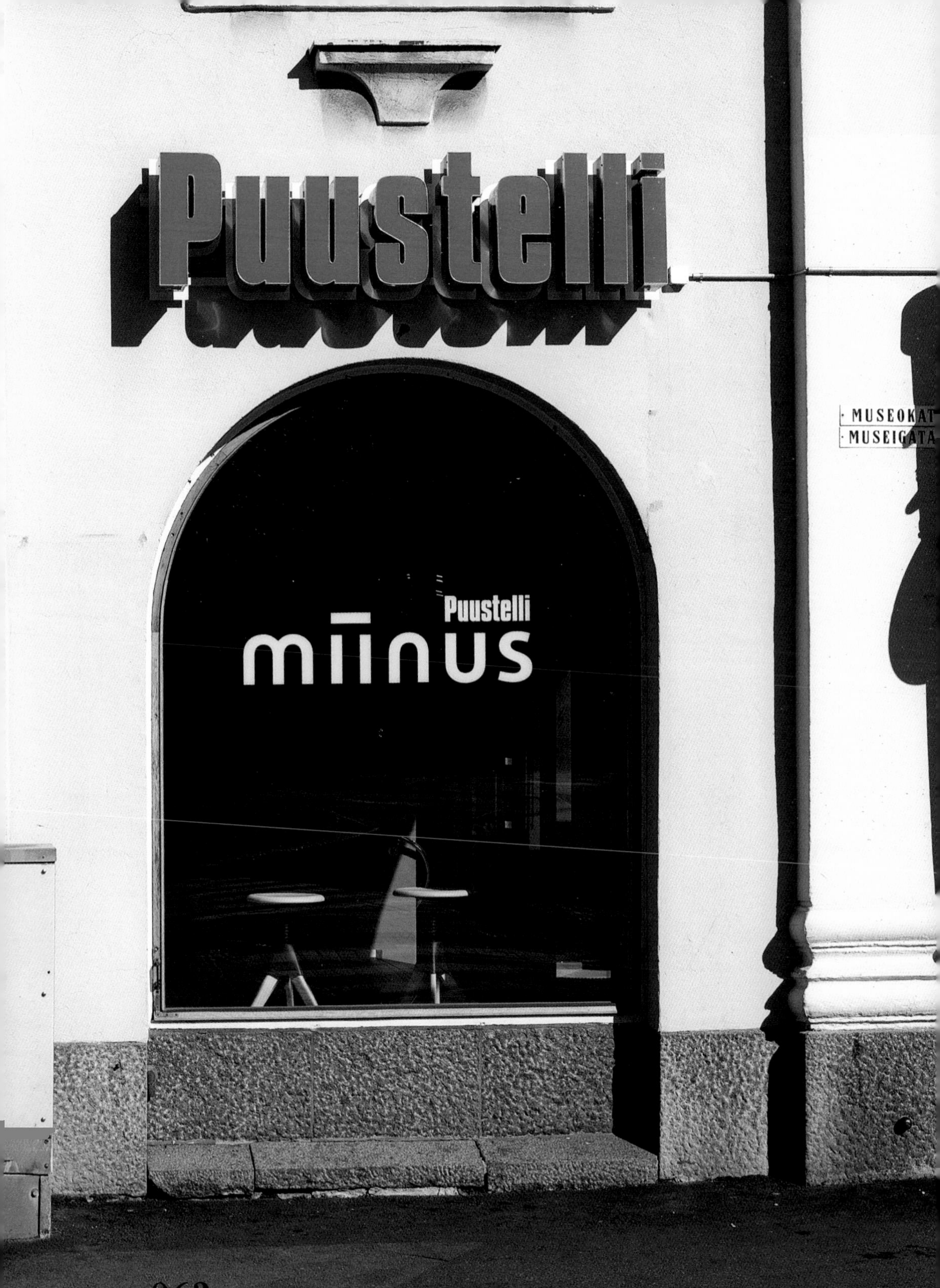
Puustelli
MUSEOKAT
MUSEIGATA
Puustelli
miinus

PIZZA
SUSHI
CAFÉ

ESTE
OESTE

BELÉM · LISBOA

Le Pari's

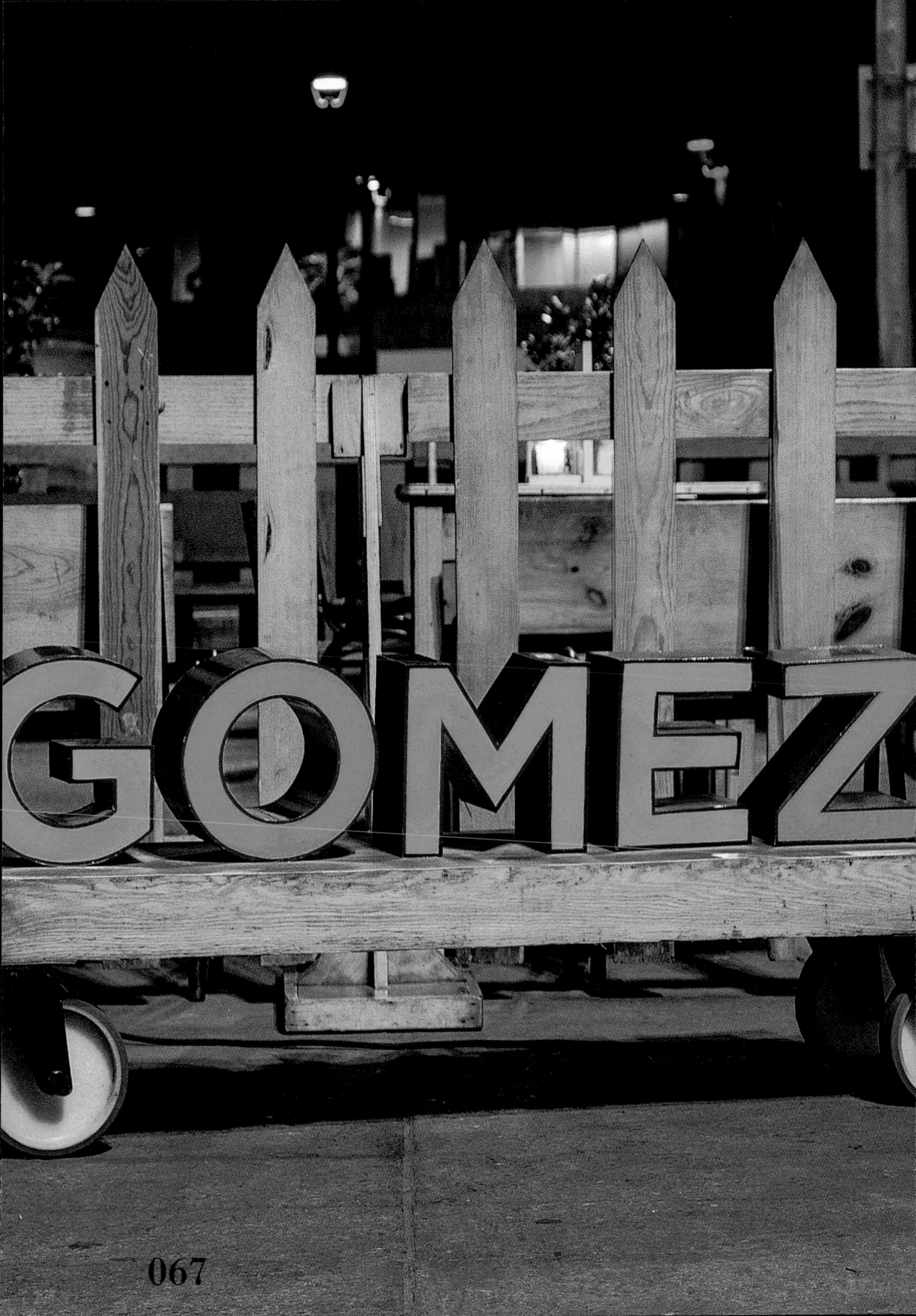
GOMEZ

THERE! IT'S ALRIGHT IF YOU'RE GOING **Do**NUTS

GOING DoNUTS MAKES YOU SMILE

IF YOU NEED ME EVERY DAY YOU ARE GOING DoNUTS

TOILETS →

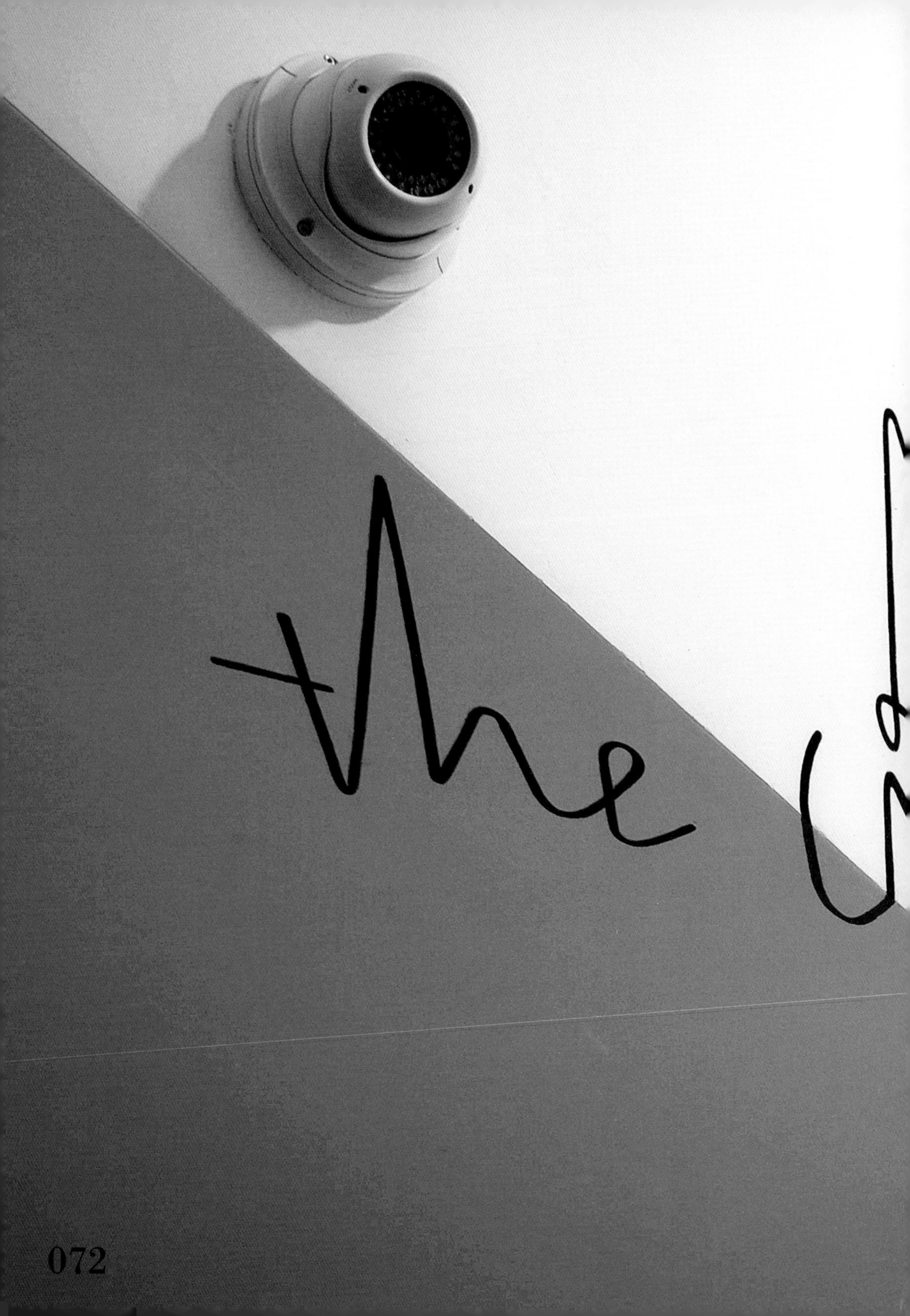
the

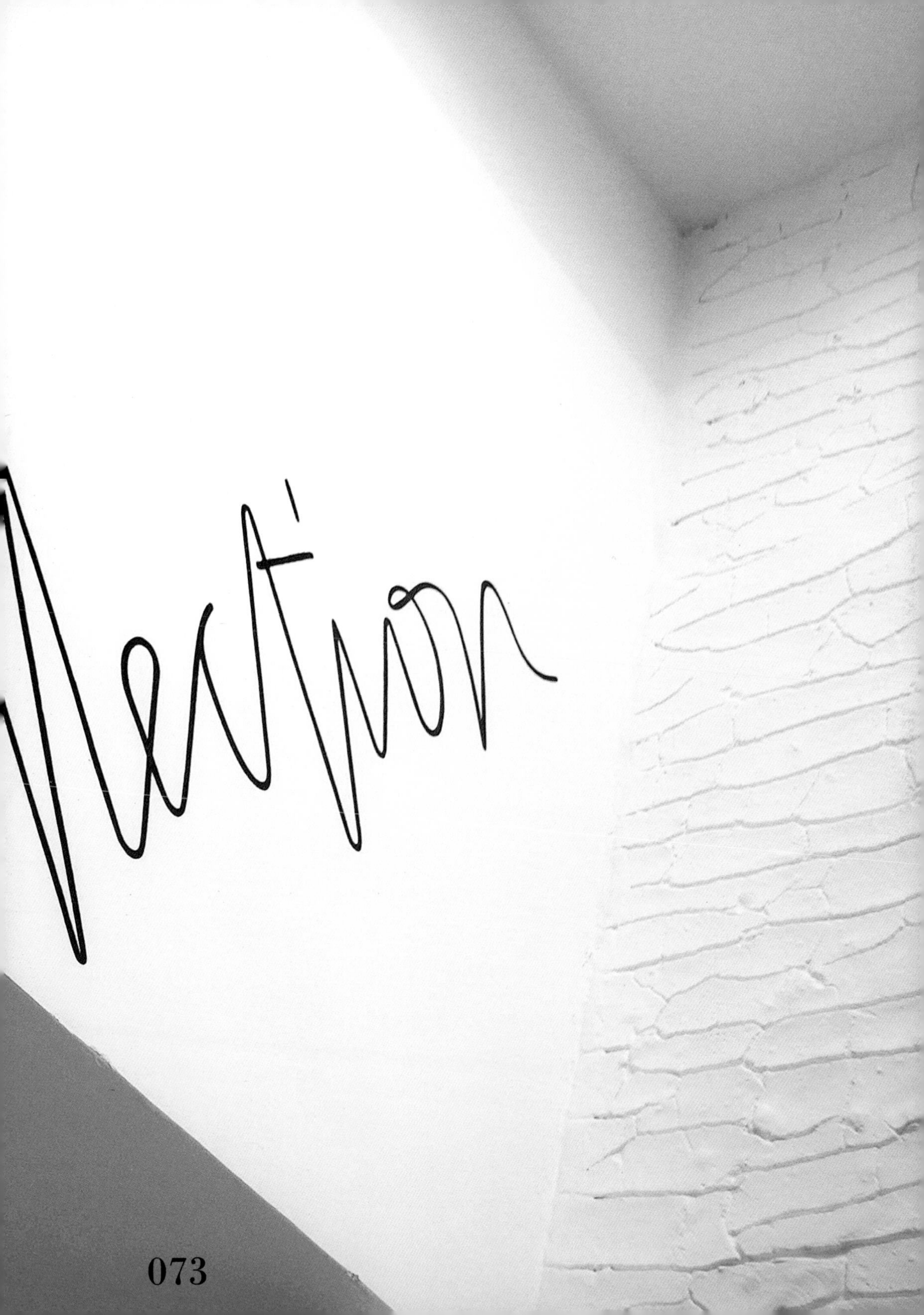

75

077

JASMINE GREEN TEA

JASMINE GREEN TEA

JASMINE GREEN TEA

JASMINE GREEN TEA

PERFECTIO
AWAITS AT
THE END OF
A STRAW

£2.95   **Large Cup**   £3.45   **Toppings**   50p   **Hot Teas**   50p
      (700ml)   (Each)   (Extra)

STRAWBERRY NECTAR   HONEYDEW MELON NECTAR   WINTERMELON NECTAR   STRAWBERRY NECTAR   PEACH NECTAR   MANGO NECTAR   LYCHEE NECTAR   LYCHEE NECTAR   CHAI NECTAR   STRAWBERRY NECTAR   MANGO NECTAR   PEACH NECTAR   STRAWBERRY NECTAR   WINTERMELON NECTAR   PINEAPPLE

Hot surface

ETE ▶ REBANADA

ачку

ve IRIS

42
AVERAGE AVOCADOS LAID PER/HR

3 SHAKES OF PEPPER
+
2 SHAKES OF SALT

HIVES = PERFECT RATI
NATOES

NK TWICE   GENTLE SLOPE
              = NO BRUISING

HIGH POWER BLEND

PRECISION BLADES

3 CLOVES OF GAR

2 SECONDS FLAT

THE AVOCADOS
PITTED + PARED

LIGHT TOSS

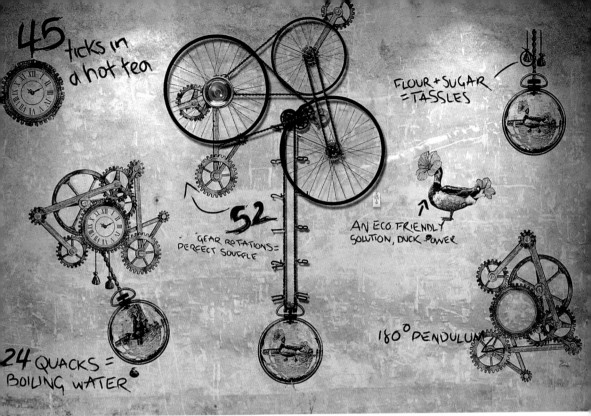

45 ticks in a hot tea

FLOUR + SUGAR = TASSLES

52

GEAR ROTATIONS = PERFECT SOUFFLE

AN ECO FRIENDLY SOLUTION, DUCK POWER

180° PENDULUM

24 QUACKS = BOILING WATER

MODEL A / 0005
DUCK RUBBER

AN ECO FR
SOLUTION DU

Bebidas

	1,00€
	1,00€
	1,00€
REFRESCO 400 cl.	1,70€
AGUA MINERAL	1,95€
CERVEZA	
REFRESCO BOTELLA 500 cl.	
VINO TINTO	

Milkshakes

Batidos fríos con base de leche natural y cremoso helado. Terminados con nata montada.

	2,75€
	2,75€
FRESA	2,75€
VAINILLA	2,75€
CHOCOLATE	2,75€
KITKAT	
OREO	

Postres

Nuestras recetas "Made in America".

MUFFIN	
DONUT	
COOKIE	
HOT ICE CREAM COOKIE	
BROWNIE (De chocolate con helado)	
TARTA CHOCOLATE	
CHEESE CAKE	
CARROT CAKE	

Helados

Nuestro cremoso helado de leche

CONO HELADO

VASO HELADO (Elige un topping)
Chocolate, Caramelo, Frutos del bosque, Almendras, Kit kat M&M's, Muesly

TOPPING EXT

	1,00€
	2,55€
	3,55€
	2,85€
	+ 0,50€
	6,85€
	+ 0,50€

Coffee Bar

Nuestras recetas de café Nespresso.

ESPRESSO	1,10€
CORTADO	1,20€
CAFÉ LATTE	1,40€
CAPUCCINO	1,60€
MOKACCINO	1,90€

Pídelo frío   + 0,20€

5€
25€
25€
,95€
2,65€
2,65€
2,65€
2,65€

the Fitzgerald ™

*La calidad se hace esperar,
¡así que ten paciencia!*

*Ofrecemos únicamente ingredientes Premium, frescos y naturales,
cocinados al momento y a la brasa de carbón de encina.*

GOURMET FAST FOOD
FLAME GRILL

1,00€
2,00€

+ 0,30€

CARDINAL CAFÉ

095

SWEE T

T REAT

Kaffe, the
og butik

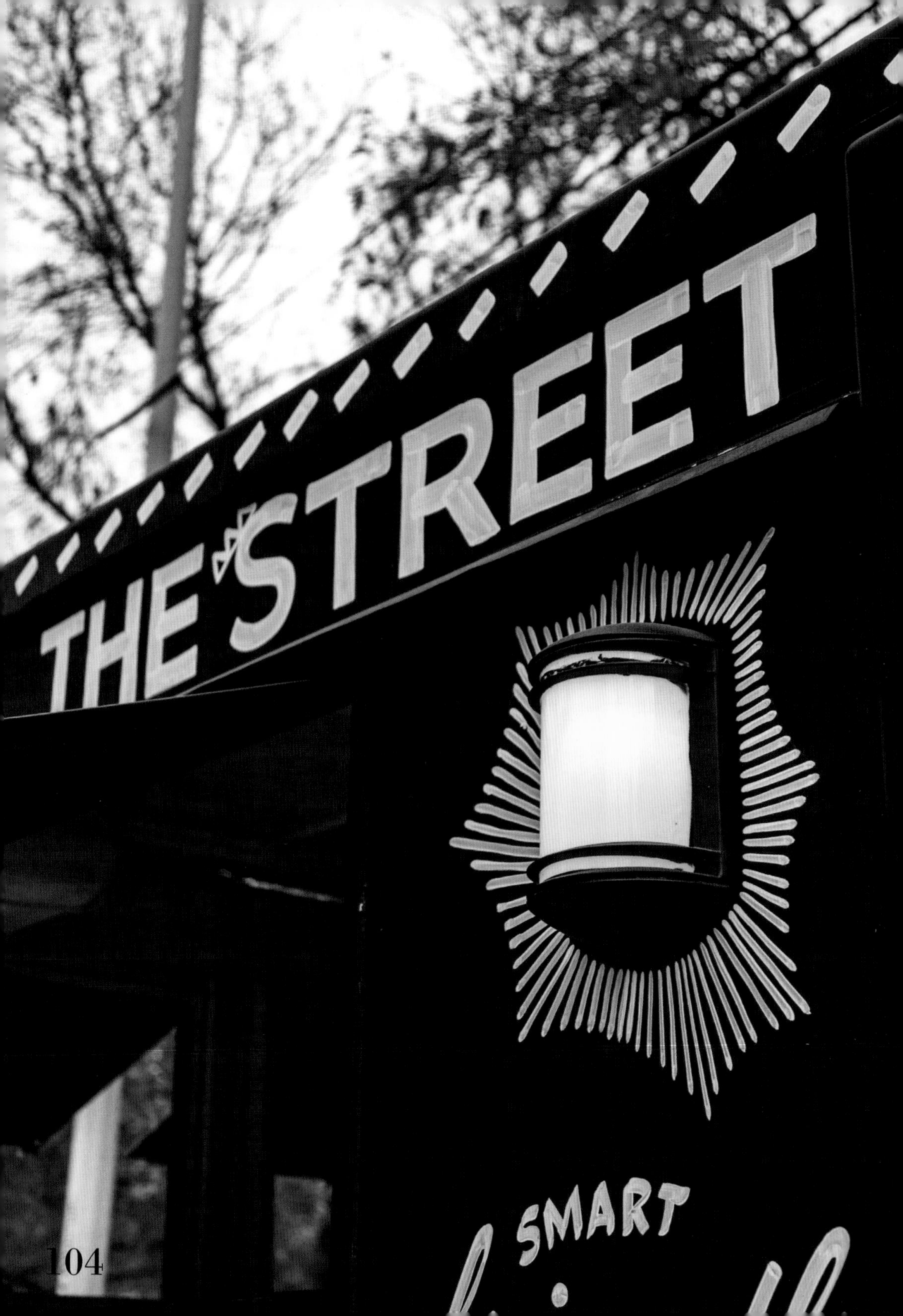
THE STREET
SMART

SMART
friendly
FOOD

 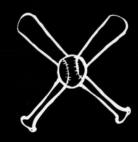 

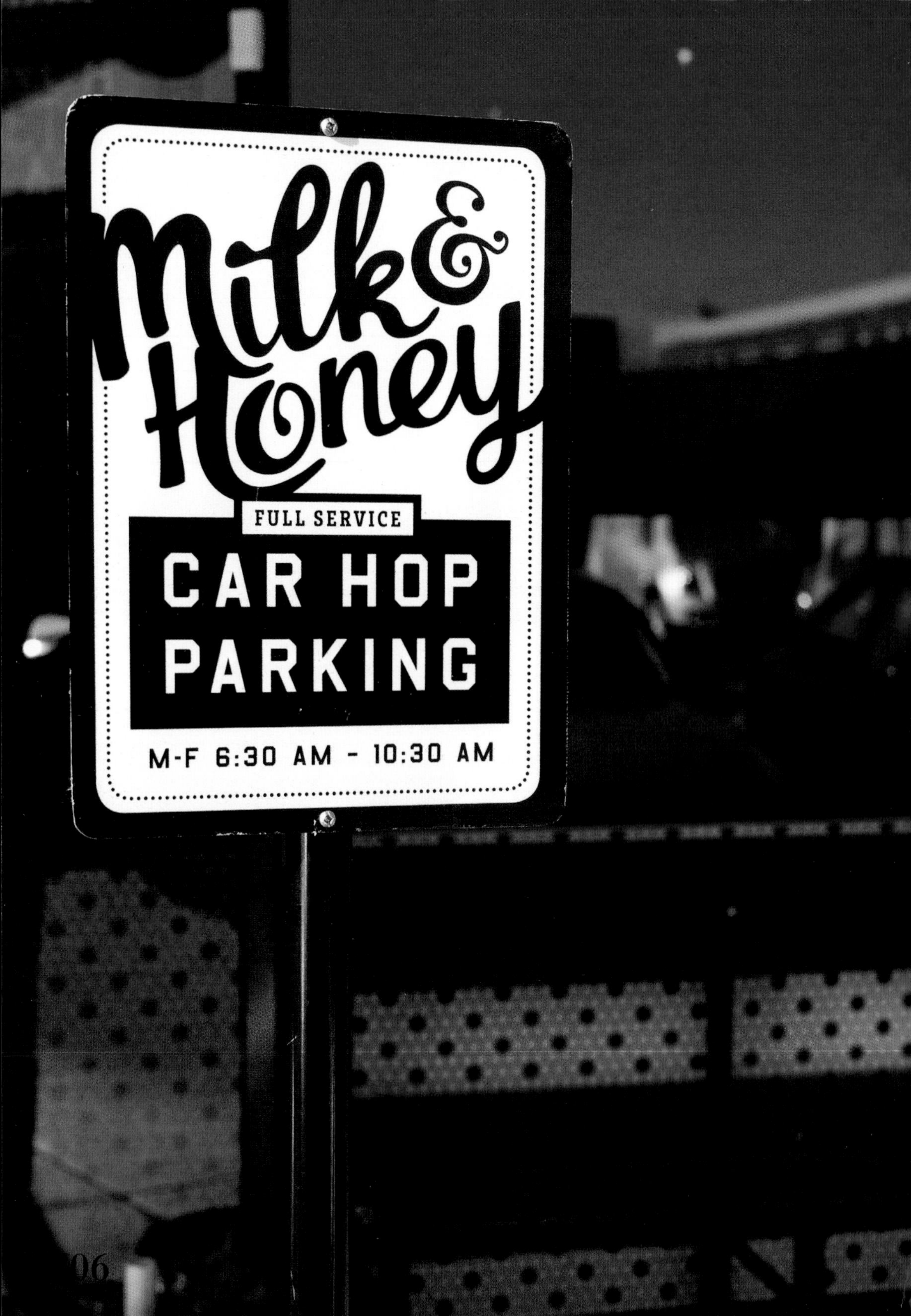
Milk &
Honey
FULL SERVICE
CAR HOP
PARKING
M-F 6:30 AM - 10:30 AM

OUTPOST
Nº 903™
GASTROBAR

TRADING HOURS
Mondays, Wednesdays, Thursdays: 3pm to 12am
Fridays, Saturdays & Eve of Public Holidays: 3pm to 3am
Sundays & Public Holidays: 10am to 12am

FIND US ON FACEBOOK
Outpost 903 Gastrobar

ENQUIRIES/RESERVATIONS
+65 6468 4903

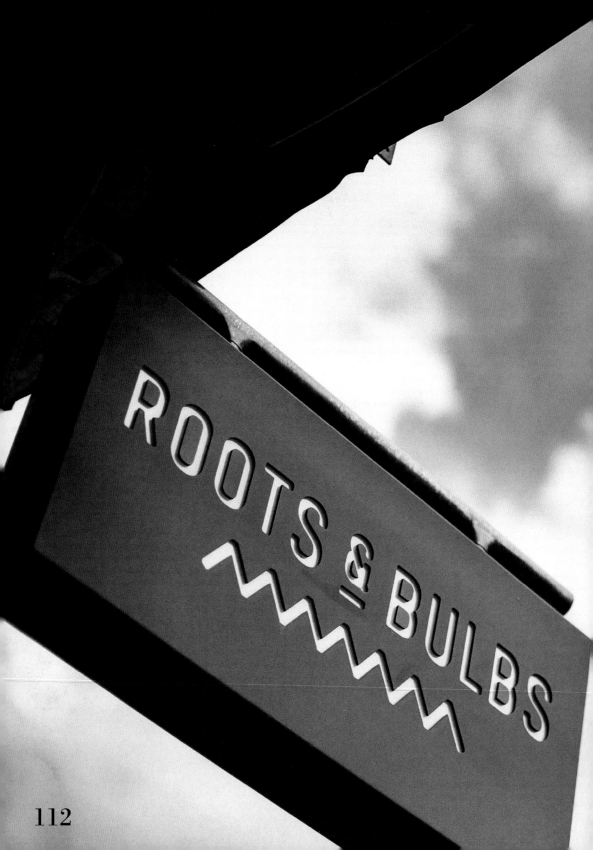

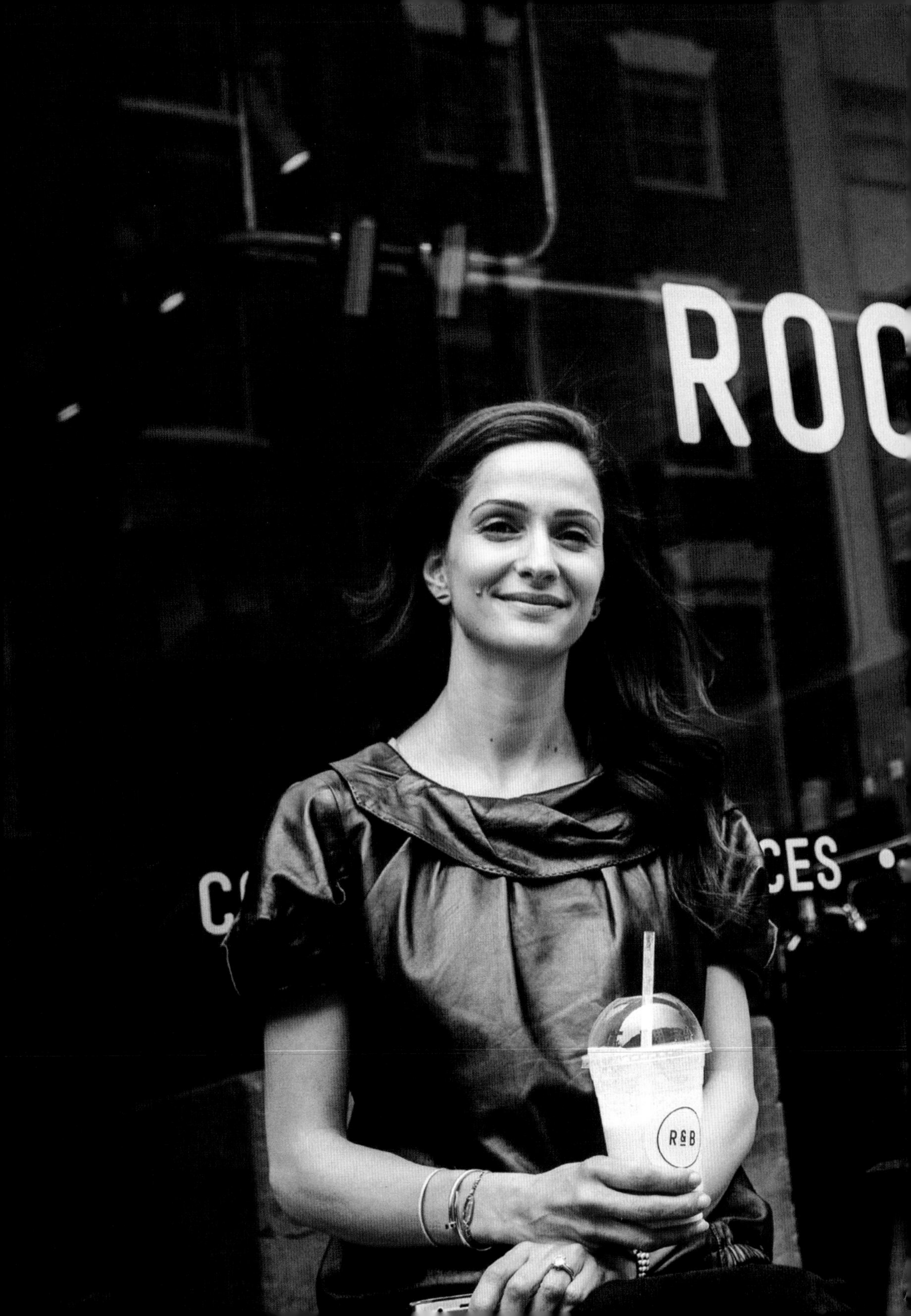
R&B

S & BULBS
Our system
G2 G3
Fruitier
C1 C2 C3
The higher the number the sweeter the taste.
PERFOOD SMOOTHIES • WHOLESOME ORGANIC

116

Tomás

Tomás

Casa Editora de Té

En Tomás estamos convencidos de que el té es una experiencia de aroma y sabor que se traduce en bienestar para el cuerpo y la mente. Congruentes con esta filosofía, en Tomás sólo seleccionamos una distinguida variedad de tés cultivados por manos artesanas que transmiten la historia, tradición y cultura de su lugar de procedencia.

Relaja tus sentidos y acompáñanos. Bienvenido.

Sean realistas,
pidan lo imposible

MAHL CAFÉ·DELI

HANDWERK
& QUALITÄT WERK

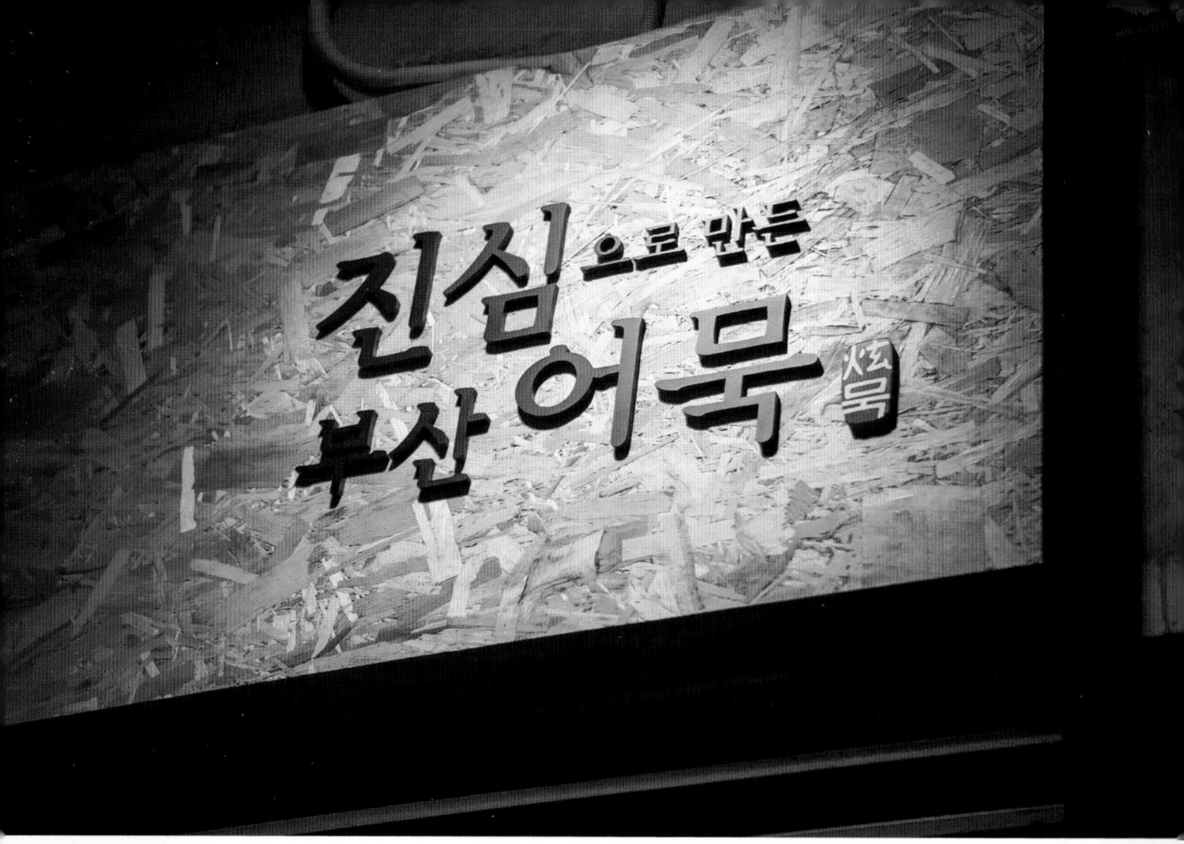

진심으로 만든
부산 어묵 쌤묵

10:00 AM ~ 08:00 PM
매주 일요일은 정기휴무입니다.
www.fishncake.com | 02.501.7184

124

125

SUSHIT

NIGIRI

TAMAGO	5,00€
LOHI	5,00€
RAPU	4,50€
ANKKA	5 00€

MAKI

KURKKU	5,00€
MANGO	5,00€
LOHI	5,50€

INSIDE OUT:

- SESAM
- SPICY

LOHI	10,50€
RAPU	10,50€
KANA	10,50€

SUSHILAJITELMAT

8 PALAA 11,00€
12 PALAA 15,00€

RIISIPAPERIRULLAT

PARSA	4,00€
LOHI	4,50€
KANA	4,00€
ANKKA	4,00€

TERIYAKI

... ...LAATTI 12,00€

ETHOS
DELICIOUSLY DIFFERENT

ETHOS
DELICIOUSLY DIFFERENT

129

itsu
soups & sushi

If a potnoodle died and went to heaven
it would surely come back as a Potsu™

Julian Metcalfe

itsu

soups & sushi

ARTISAN
PASTA

MOUSTACHE-LICKING GOOD

HANDMADE S
BY ITALIANS

KARAWAY

Welcome to Karaw
a difference. The
how we bake and
The difference is i

134

First come, first served

First come, first served

I'm a Koodoo man

Fast as lightning

I ♥ Koodoo

I'm a Koodoo man

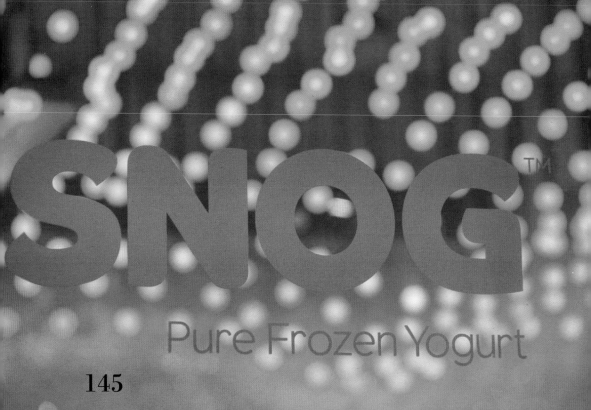

STREETZ
AMERICAN GRILL

CHICAGO DOG

PHILLY STEAKS AND GYROS

Philly Cheese Steak Sandwich $6.95

Grilled rib-eye steak on a fresh Italian roll "wit'" onions or wit'out." Cheez Whiz®, provolone or American cheese.

Grilled peppers? Add mushrooms?

$6.95

149

IF YOU LIKE SUSHI
YOU'LL LOVE TEMAKI

Yoobi is proud to be
London's first temakeria.

SEASONAL
SALADS

HOT
SOUPS

REFRESHING
TEAS

FRESH
JUICES

GÖTG
STORI

ESPRESSO
22/26:-

CAPPUCCINO
28:-

**FÄRSKMAL
BRYGGKAF**
26:-

MACCHIATO
24/28:-

CAFFE LATTE
34:-

STORMVARNING

SVART &
FRUKTIGT

EARL GREY

SVART &
AROMATISKT

SÖDERMALMS-
BLANDNING

SÖTAKTIG SMAK

BLÅBÄR

SVART &
EKOLOGISKT

LUST & FÄGRING

GRÄDDIGT MED
SOLROSBLAD,
MANGO OCH
HALLON

ROOIBOS VANILJ

RÖTT TE
SMAKSATT MED
VANILJ
KOFFEINFRITT

ATAN
ES

LÖSVIKTSTE
26:-

BLOMTE
34:-

BIODYNAMISK
JUICE
28:-

EKOLOGISK
SMOOTHIE
34:-

BER

& SVENSK

CHAI

SVART &
KRYDDIGT

CITRUS

SYRLIGT &
FAIRTRADE

EARL GREEN

GRÖNT TE MED
CITRON -OCH
LIMESMAK

153

160

SOAP TOWELS

ice cream
factory

163

165

WHOPPER BAR BK

BK WHOPPER™ BAR

WHOPPER YOUR WAY™

BK WHOPPER
BAR
WORLD'S FIRST

IT STARTED AS A SPARK.
IT SPREAD INTO AN INFERNO.
100% FLAME-BROILED BEEF,
TOPPED WITH UNIQUE INGREDIENTS.
AMERICA'S FAVORITE BURGER, WITH
MORE THAN A MILLION WAYS TO
HAVE IT YOUR WAY.

HOT CHOCOLATE

	PRIMO	MEDIO	MASSIMO
HOT CHOCOLATE	2.15	2.45	2.65
WITH MARSHMALLOWS & WHIPPED CREAM	2.55	2.85	3.05
WITH WHIPPED CREAM & CHOCOLATE STICK	2.70	3.00	3.20

ICED TEA

	PRIMO	MEDIO
RASPBERRY ICED TEA	2.00	2.30
PEACH ICED TEA	2.00	2.30

ICED COFFEE

	PRIMO	MEDIO
ICED LATTE / ICED CAPPUCCINO	2.10	2.40
ICED SPECIALITY LATTE	2.40	2.70
ICED MOCHA	2.30	2.60

ICE COLD COSTA

	PRIMO	MEDIO
FRESCATO		
COFFEE	2.75	3.05
MOCHA	2.95	3.25
FRUIT COOLER		
RED BERRY	2.90	3.10
MANGO & PASSIONFRUIT	2.90	3.10
SICILIAN LEMONADE	2.90	3.10
ICE DESSERTS		
SIMPLY VANILLA	2.75	3.05
STRAWBERRY SHORTCAKE	3.05	3.35
DOUBLE CHOCOLATE FLAKE	3.05	3.35

RELAX

AS – 35p eac
SHOT OF SYRUP
SHOT OF ESPRESSO
LATE FLAK
LATE STICK
ED CREAM
MALLOWS

PECIAL REQUESTS?
wing are availa le at no extra charge
einated coff
ned or soya

FREE
WiFi

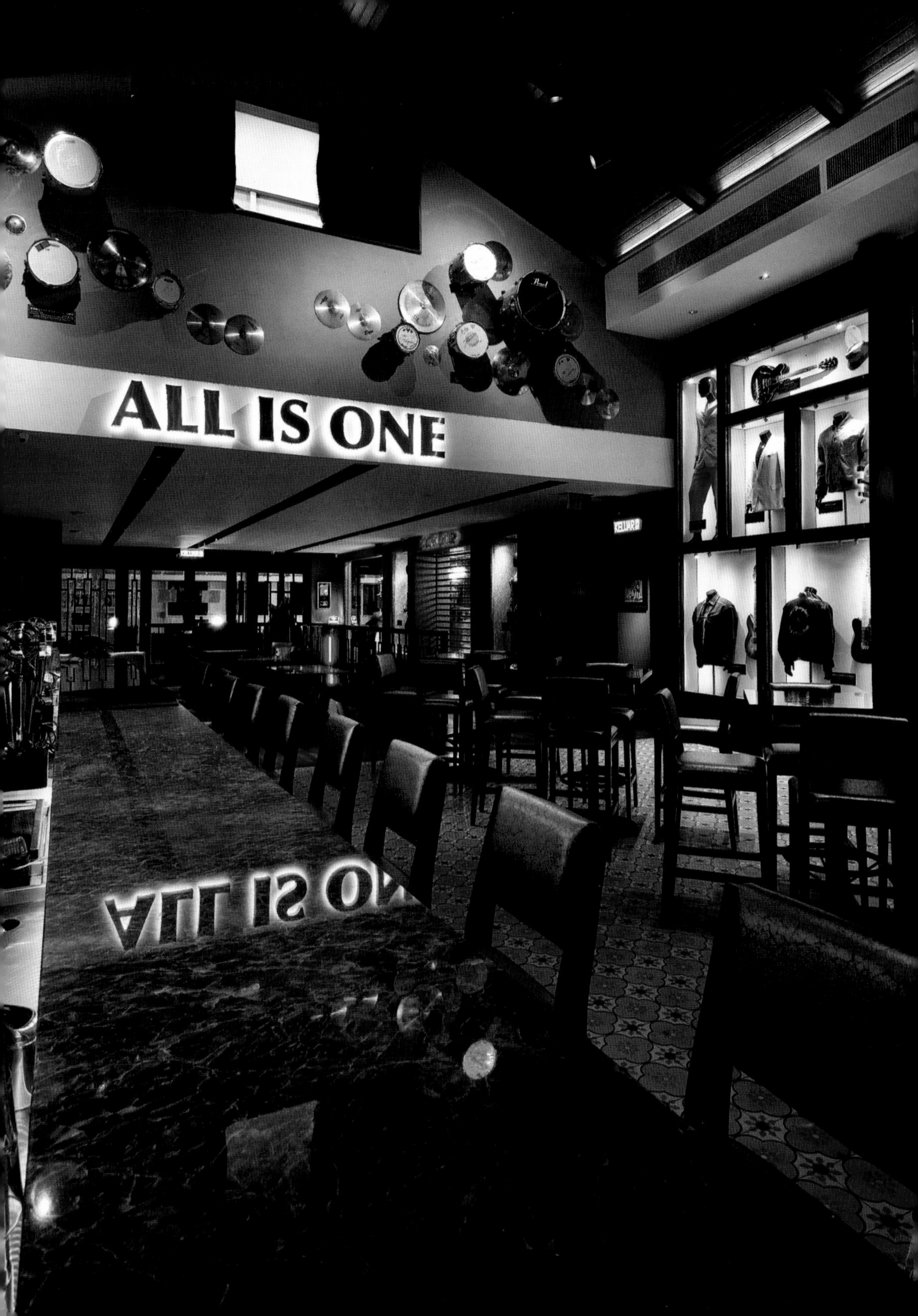
ALL IS ONE
KELUAR

181

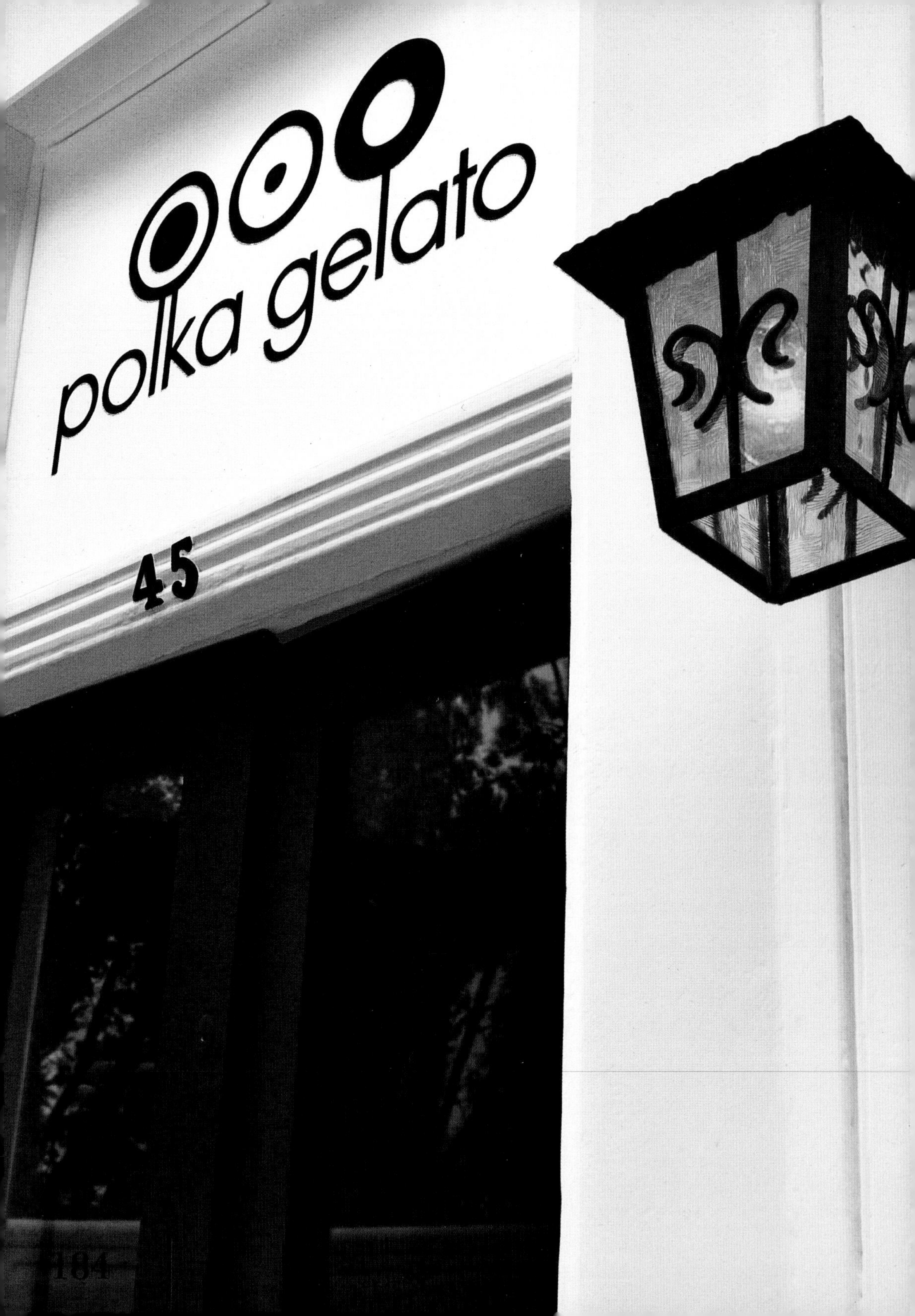
polka gelato
45

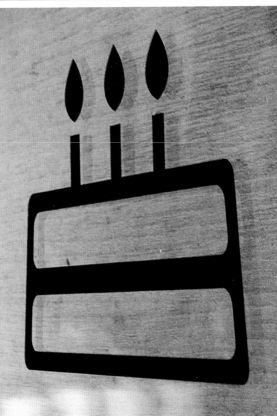

187

189

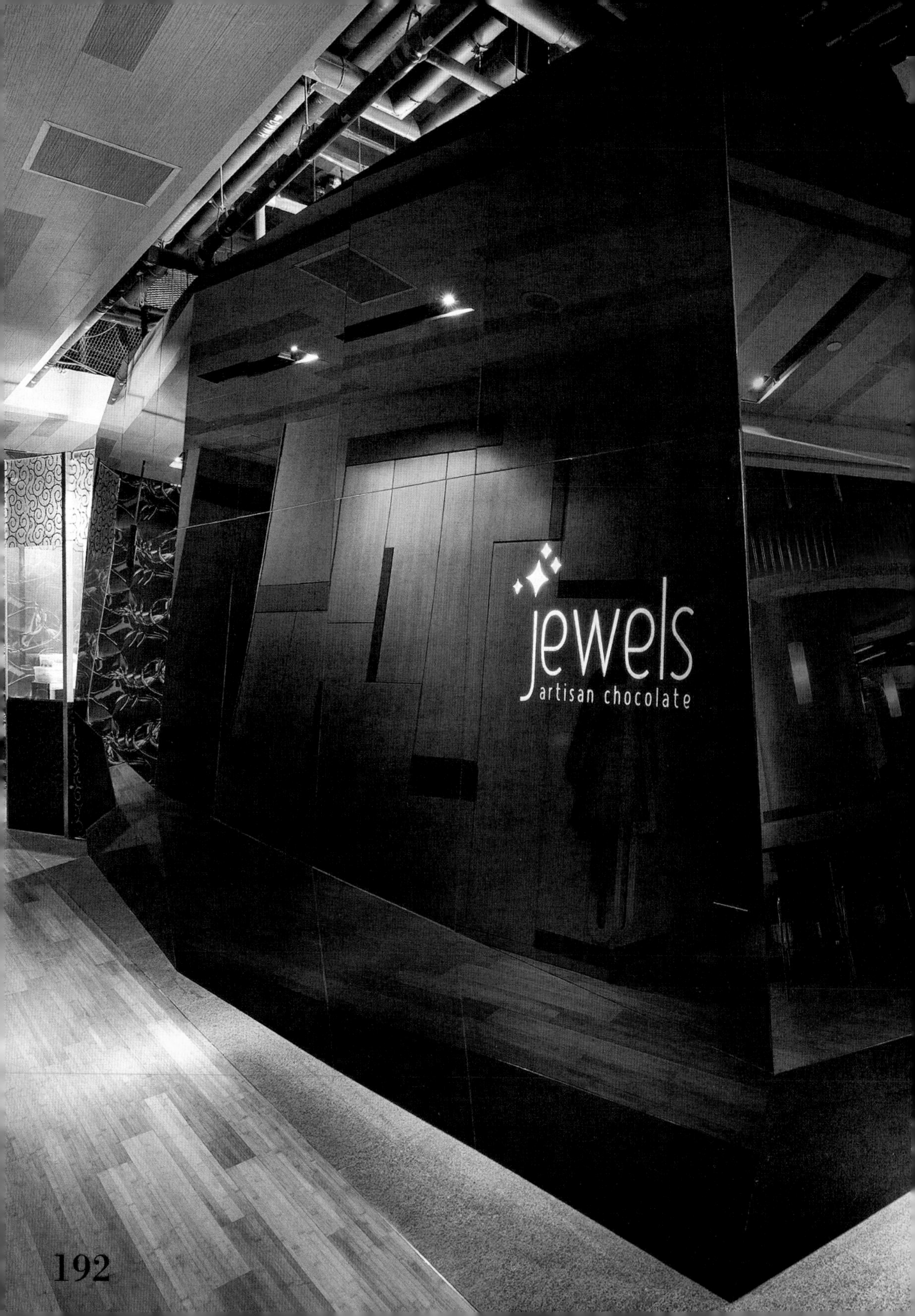
jewels
artisan chocolate

193

10 BASIC MEDITERRANEAN

DIET RECOMMENDATIONS

Use olive oil as your main
source of added fat.

Eat plenty of plant-based foods. For
dessert, eat fresh fruit on
a daily basis.

Bread and other cereal foods should
be a part of your everyday diet.

Fresh, locally produced and in-season
foods that have undergone minimal
processing are best.

Consume dairy products on a daily
basis.

Red meat should be consumed in
moderation.

Eat plenty of fish, but eggs in
moderation.

Water is the beverage par excellence
in the Mediterranean. Wine should be
taken in moderations and with meals.
Be physically active every day.

**Be physically active
every day.**

THIS IS OUR STORY

We turned to organic farming and its
natural and healthy lifestyle after
some health problems in our family,
caused by intensive crop cultivation
practices.

We found our haven in the Alpujarra
region of the province of Almería
(South East Spain), and El Cortijo El
Cura became one of Spain's pioneering
organic farms.

Situated in Laujar de Andarax, a village
steeped in history and tradition, our
family business aims to develop
sustainably within the framework of
this rich local legacy.

The views from our farm are
breathtaking, the magical sunsets over
the Sierra Nevada mountain range
painting a background to unique and
unforgettable Mediterranean flavours.

Our farm, our philosophy and our
pleasure. We hand you over to your
experience.

The Sánchez Vizcaíno family.

BALZAC

BRASSERIE

BALZAC

BALZAC

BRASSERIE

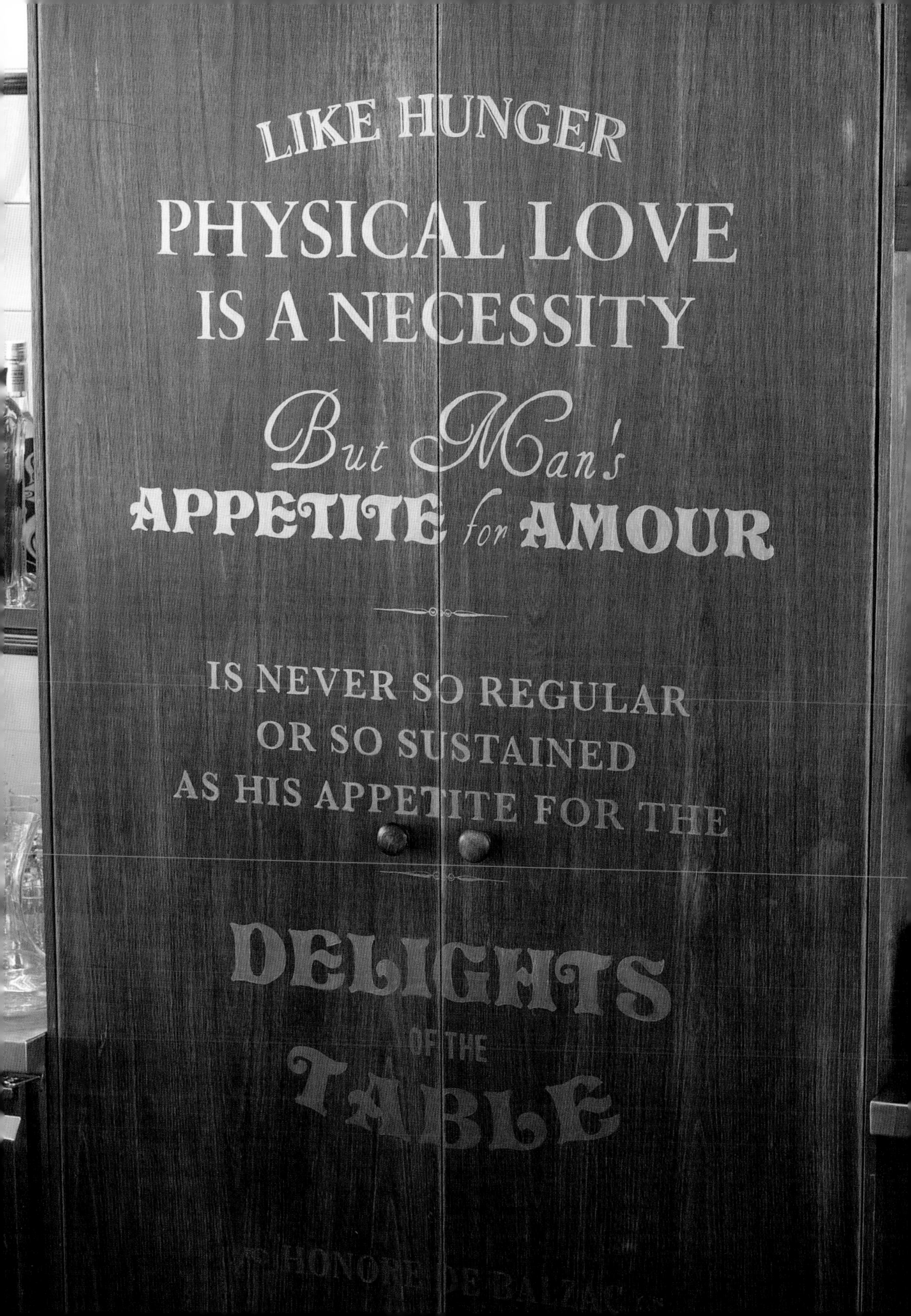

LIKE HUNGER

PHYSICAL LOVE
IS A NECESSITY

But Man's
APPETITE *for* AMOUR

IS NEVER SO REGULAR
OR SO SUSTAINED
AS HIS APPETITE FOR THE

DELIGHTS
OF THE
TABLE

HONORÉ DE BALZAC

LES SALADES

LES TARTINES
GOURMANDES

PAIN
TRADITIONNEL

PODI

THE FOOD ORCHARD

CUCINA & BAR

SOPRA

CUCINA & BAR
SOPRA
ZIONALE SARDA
ITALIAN PIZZA
APERITIV
PROSECCO
FORMA

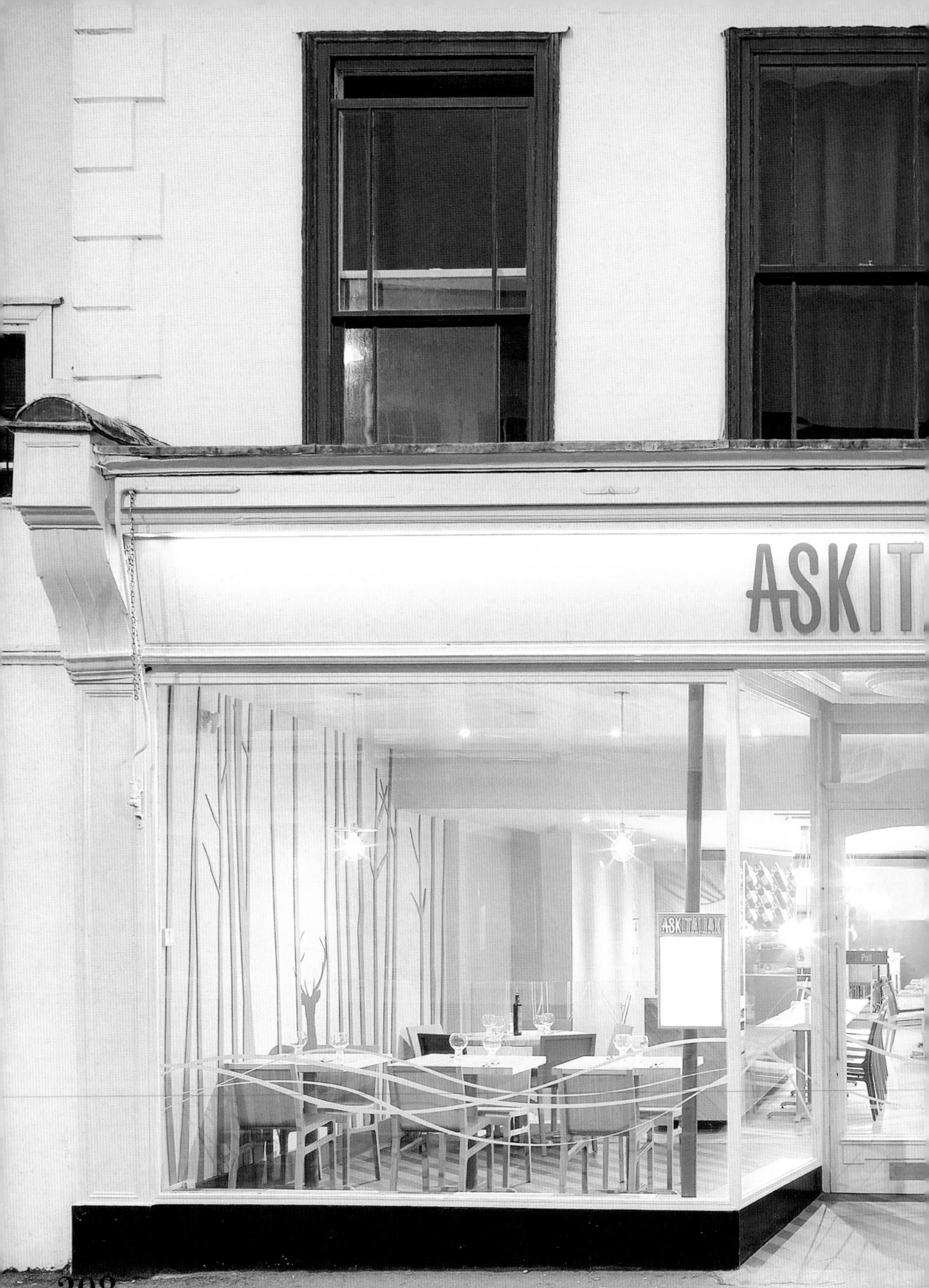
ASKIT
ASKITALIAN
Pull

209

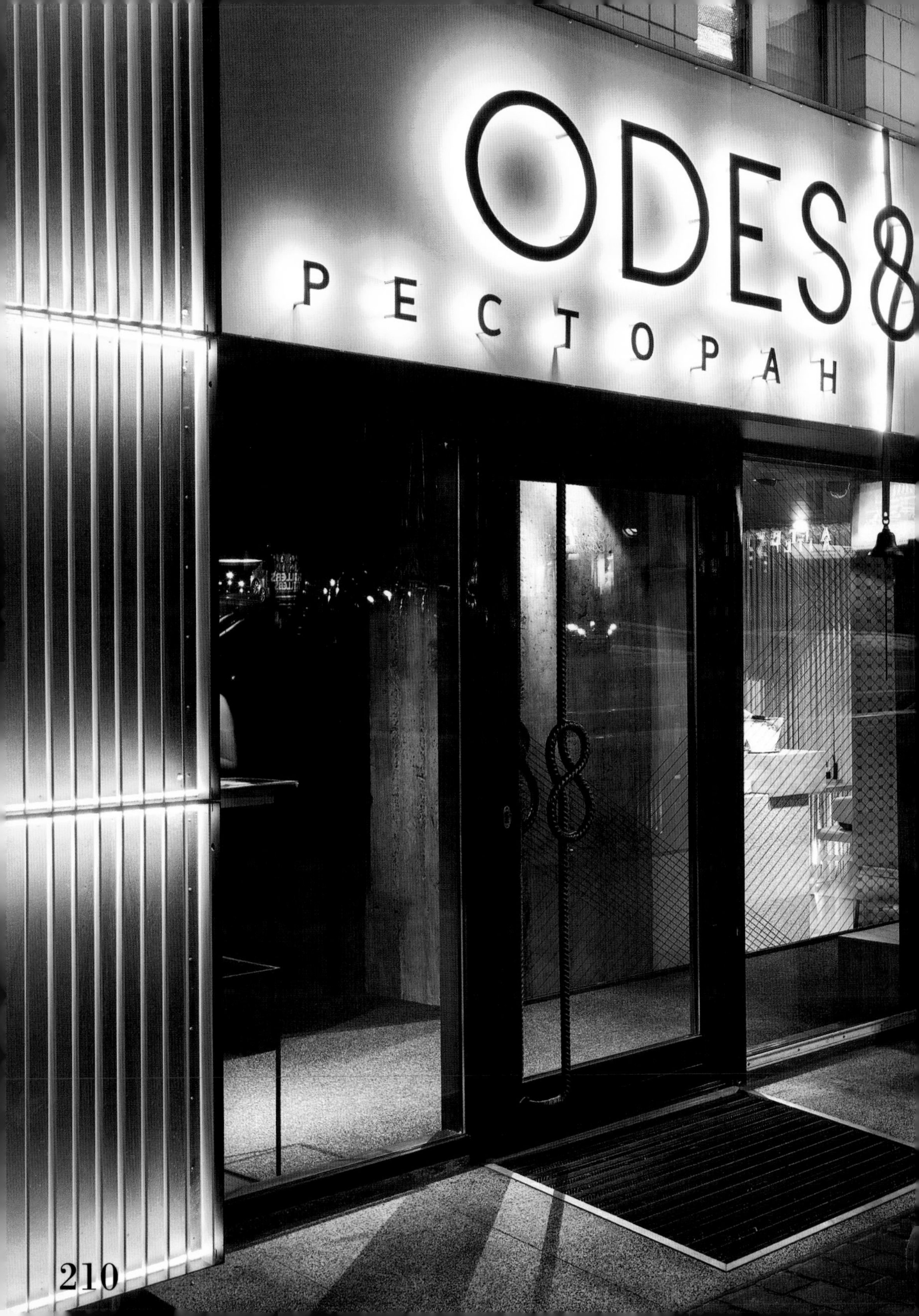
ODES8
РЕСТОРАН

SALA DE DESPIECE

C/ PONZANO

HORARIO

CONTACTO

SERVICIOS

GRAN DEGUSTACIÓN

Heineken

Heineken

GRAN
DEGUSTACIÓN

212

213

215

GIORNO

TRATTORIA/BAR

219

rสืพสรdeLight
by ...

焼鳥
炭地野菜
地地

と〻と〻

227

229

take a moment to plan your day

TEMPO

TEMPO
patisserie & cafe

12:00 taste
a breakout

14:00 lay down
for a while

231

TV

22:01 throw the tv out the window

23:23 enjoy the city lights

22:05 grab your gear

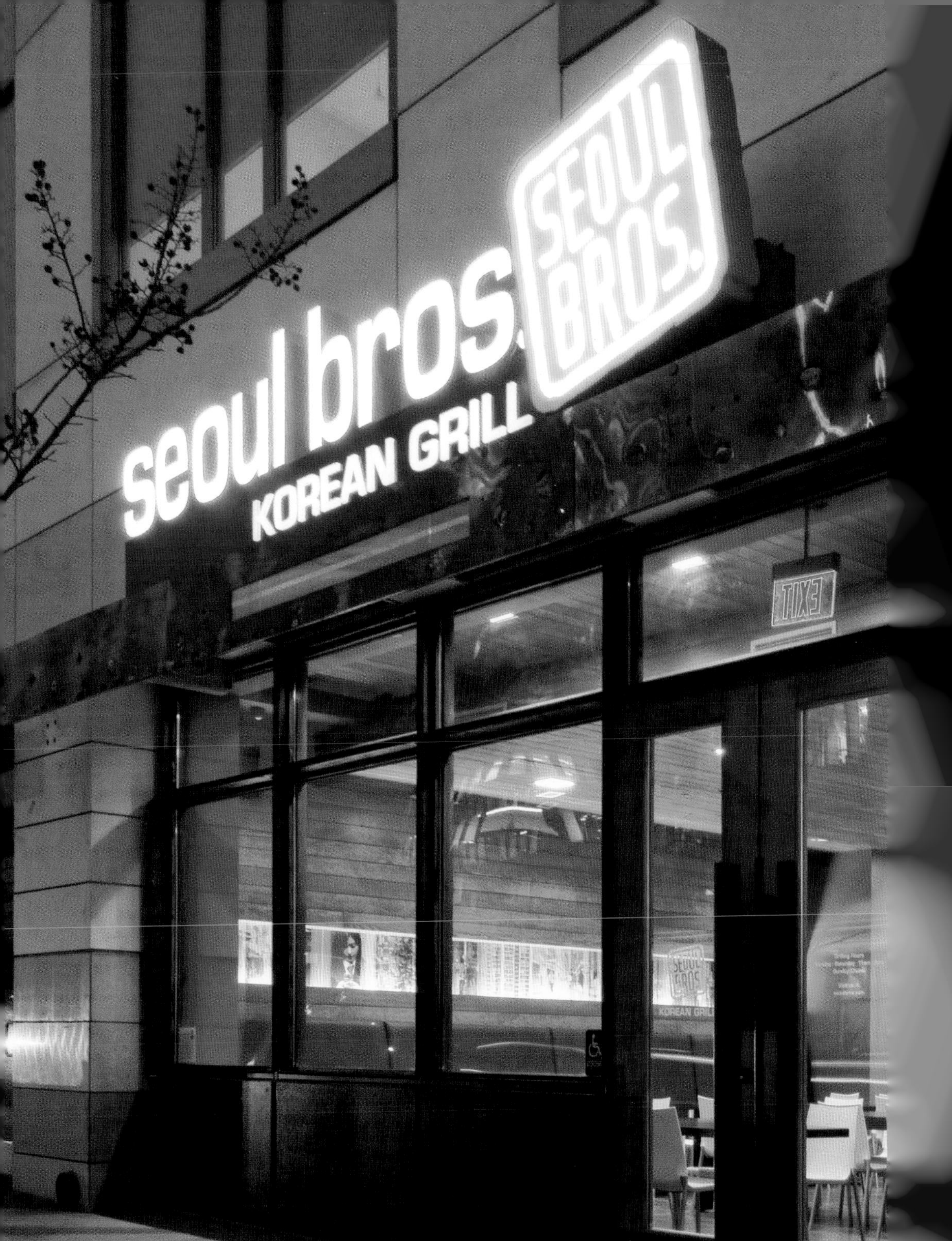
seoul bros.
KOREAN GRILL
SEOUL BROS.
EXIT

241

TWENTY FIVE LUSK

25

43

245

CAFE DEL ARCO

Tiempo en España
Martes 22 de diciembre

252

JAPANESE BISTRO and TAPAS

JAPANESE

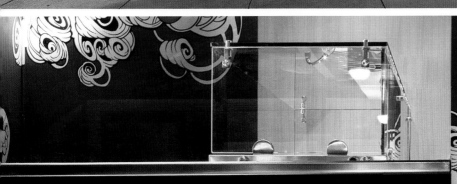

VILLA PLANCHA

Restaurant
VILLA
PLANCHA
Cuisine Ensoleillée

271

De farine & d'eau fraiche

BOULANGERIE ITALIANA

PUSATERI'S

277

279

ASCHAN
— CAFÉ JUGEND —

PÄIVÄN MENU

TOMAATTI-VUOHENJUUSTOKEITTO
UUNIPERUNA, 3 TÄYTEVAIHTOEHTOA
SALAATTEJA

 KAHVIA – KAFFE
COFFEE

 VIINIÄ – VIN
WINE

 SYÖTÄVÄÄ – MAT
FOOD

 TAPAKSIA – TAPAS
TAPAS

 KUOHUVAA – SKUMMANDE
SPARKLING

 MAKEAA – SÖT
SWEET

 LUKEMISTA – LÄSNING
TO READ

 SALONKI – SALONG
LOUNGE

 PUISTONÄKYMÄ – PARK VY
PARK VIEW

 LIIKUNTARAJOITTEISILLE
HANDIKAPPAD – HANDICAPPED

 NAISILLE – DAMER
LADIES

 MIEHILLE – MÄN
GENTS

OLET TÄSSÄ - DU ÄR HÄR
YOU ARE HERE

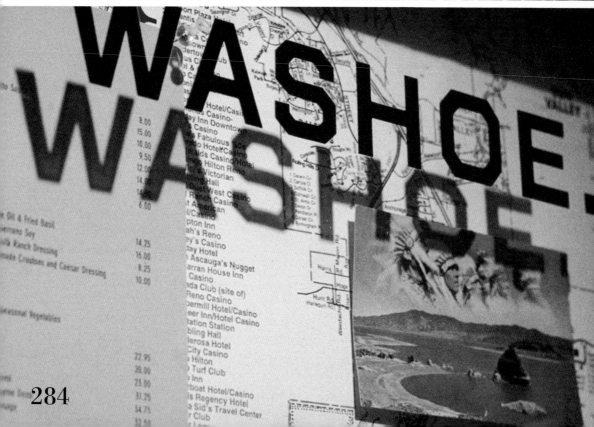

284

287

288

289

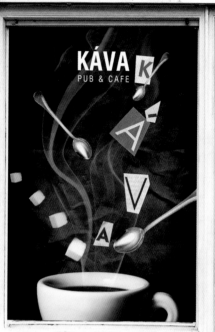

KÁVA
PUB & CAFE

KÁVA
PUB & CAFE

KÁVA | PUB & CAFE

LA SELVA

291

AVE THE EDGE?
ealthy, gourmet & 100% Australian

our beer battered **FRIES** are thick & supa crunchy, cooked in canola oil & come with flavoured salts & dipping sauces

our **PATTIES** are made from premium lean Australian beef, 150 grams of grilled goodness

salt & pepper

coffee's		tea's		drinks		sweets	
cappuccino	2.70	english breakfast	2.80	cold drinks		cakes	
latte	2.90	chamomile	2.80	fresh juices		danishes	
flat white	2.70	green tea	2.80	flavoured milks		european sweets	
long black espresso	2.70	bengati chal	2.80			gateaux desserts	
short black	2.40	earl grey	2.80	milkshakes	3.50	slices	
macchiato	2.40	sweet lemon and peel	2.80	thickshakes	3.70	biscuits	
vienna	3.10	peppermint	2.80	(assorted flavours available)		muffins	
vienna mocha	3.20	black tea	2.80			fruit tarts	
mocha	3.10			home made iced coffee	4.00		
hot chocolate	2.70			home made iced chocolate	4.00		
soya milk coffee	2.90						
flavoured coffee	3.50						
black tea	2.40						

Index

Kevin Wu

Kilian O'Sulivan

kissmiklos

Kyle You

Lai Siew Hong, Hanako Suzuka, Kenny Tan, Mak Sook Har

Lee Jae-yeol, Kim min-back, Kim hyun-ju

Lee Pyo-joon

Lemongraphic

Lin Ho

Lo Siento Studio

LORENC+YOO DESIGN

LOU-KWUO-CHI

Luca Bertacchi & Sara Bergami

Luciana Carvalho and Renato Diniz

Luda Galchenko

M+R interior architecture

Mantra Branding

Marcelo Donadussi

Marco Covi. Trieste (copyright Dimitri Waltritsch)

Mariano Herrera

Marina Goñi

Marion Luttenberger

Mark Horton / Architecture, Bentel & Bentel

Mark Luthringer

MASQUESPACIO

Matteo Modena

Matteo Piazza - Milan

Meanwhile

Melissa Werner

Metropolis Peru / José Orrego

Michael Kai

Michael Königshofer

Miguel de Guzmán

Mind Design

Minifie van Schaik Architects

Mizzi Studios

MM

moodley brand identity

mooof / Sunthorn Keeratayakom

Morris Selvatico

NABITO ARCHITECTS (Alessandra Faticanti, Roberto Ferlito)

Nacasa & Partners Inc.

Nathanael Hughes

NEMA Workshop

New Agency

Nick Thompson

Nota

Nota Design International Pte Ltd.

OHLAB / Paloma Hernaiz and Jaime Oliver

Olga Ruíz

Olson Kundig Architect

osé Carlos Cruz Arquitecto

Outofstock Design

P.Makridis + Associates

Paavo Lehtonen

Paul Dyer

Paul Sieka

Pereira Miguel Arquitectos, Lda.

Philip Castleton / Philip Castleton Photography Inc.,
Toronto, ON

Philippe Dureuil

Pierluigi Piu

plajer & franz studio gbr/ project gmbh

PLAYGROUND Büro für Gestaltung

Plotcreative Interior Design Limited

Preen Inc.

Pregnolato e Kusuki estúdio Fotográfico

PROCESS5 DESIGN Noriaki Takeda, Ikuma Yoshizawa,
Tatsuya Horii

Public-Library

PYO JOON, LEE

Renaud Callebaut

Re-public

Rice Creative

Richard Dean

Rien van Rijthoven

Rina Jordan

Robot Food

Rodrigo Aguadé & Manuel Astorga

Roland Persson

Rolf Ockert Design

Rui Moreira Santos, Espinho

Sandra Tarruella Interioristas

Satoru Umetsu/ Nacasa&Partners

Savvy Studio

Scott Francis

Scott McDonald & Hedrich Blessing

SEA DESIGN

SeeMeDesign, LLC

Seiryo Studio

SHH / Neil Hogan, Brendan Heath, Adam Woodward

Shia Sai Pui

Shillington College

SK+G

SKINN DESIGN

ASH. INTERGALACTIC S

WISE PUBLICATIONS
LONDON / NEW YORK / PARIS / SYDNEY / COPENHAGEN / BERLIN / MADRID / TOKYO

EXCLUSIVE DISTRIBUTORS:
MUSIC SALES LIMITED
8/9 FRITH STREET, LONDON W1D 3JB, ENGLAND.
MUSIC SALES PTY LIMITED
120 ROTHSCHILD AVENUE, ROSEBERY, NSW 2018, AUSTRALIA.

ORDER NO. AM975810
ISBN 0-7119-9719-5
THIS BOOK © COPYRIGHT 2002 BY WISE PUBLICATIONS.

NEW MUSIC ARRANGEMENTS BY JAMES DEAN.
MUSIC PROCESSED BY PAUL EWERS MUSIC DESIGN.

PRINTED IN THE UNITED KINGDOM BY
CALIGRAVING LIMITED, THETFORD, NORFOLK.

www.musicsales.com

YOUR GUARANTEE OF QUALITY:

AS PUBLISHERS, WE STRIVE TO PRODUCE EVERY BOOK
TO THE HIGHEST COMMERCIAL STANDARDS.

WHILE ENDEAVOURING TO RETAIN THE ORIGINAL
RUNNING ORDER OF THE RECORDED ALBUM, THE BOOK HAS
BEEN CAREFULLY DESIGNED TO MINIMISE AWKWARD PAGE
TURNS AND TO MAKE PLAYING FROM IT A REAL PLEASURE.

PARTICULAR CARE HAS BEEN GIVEN TO SPECIFYING
ACID-FREE, NEUTRAL-SIZED PAPER MADE FROM PULPS WHICH
HAVE NOT BEEN ELEMENTAL CHLORINE BLEACHED.

THIS PULP IS FROM FARMED SUSTAINABLE FORESTS AND
WAS PRODUCED WITH SPECIAL REGARD FOR THE ENVIRONMENT.

THROUGHOUT, THE PRINTING AND BINDING HAVE BEEN
PLANNED TO ENSURE A STURDY, ATTRACTIVE PUBLICATION
WHICH SHOULD GIVE YEARS OF ENJOYMENT.

IF YOUR COPY FAILS TO MEET OUR HIGH STANDARDS,
PLEASE INFORM US AND WE WILL GLADLY REPLACE IT.

ASH.

BURN BABY BURN

WORDS & MUSIC BY TIM WHEELER

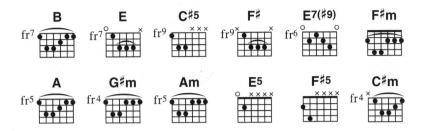

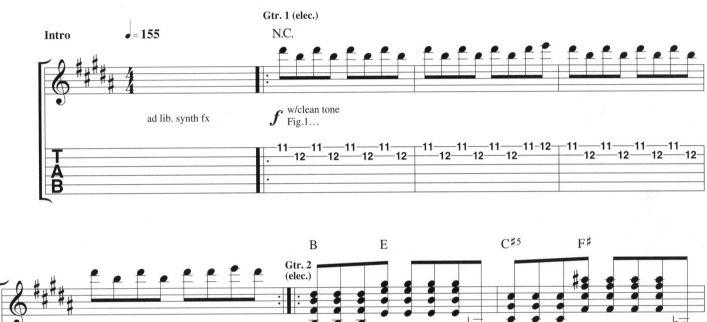

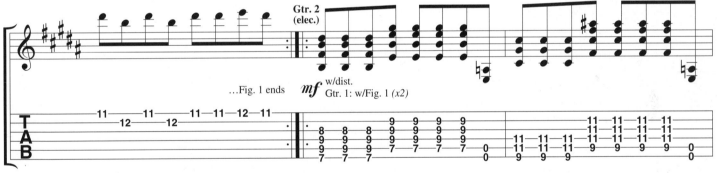

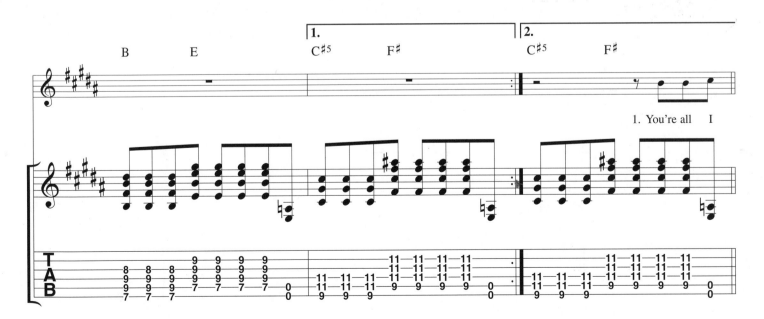

1. You're all   I

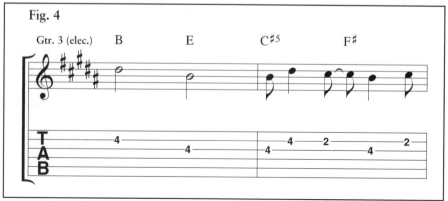

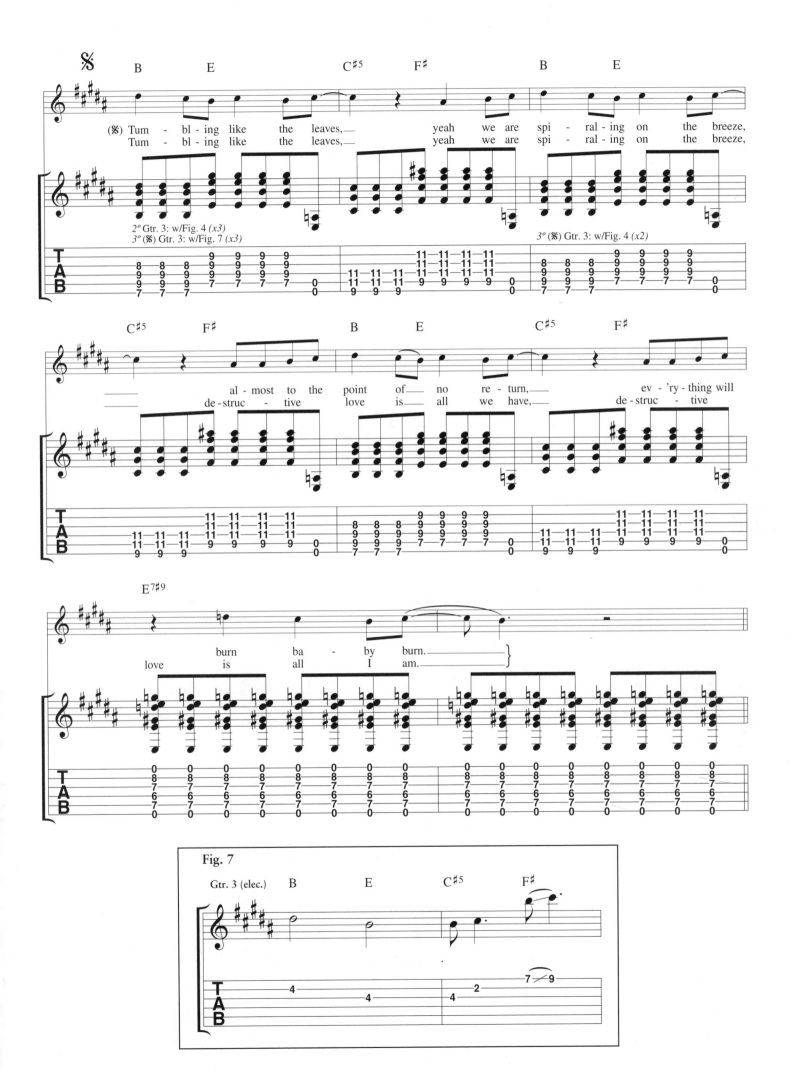

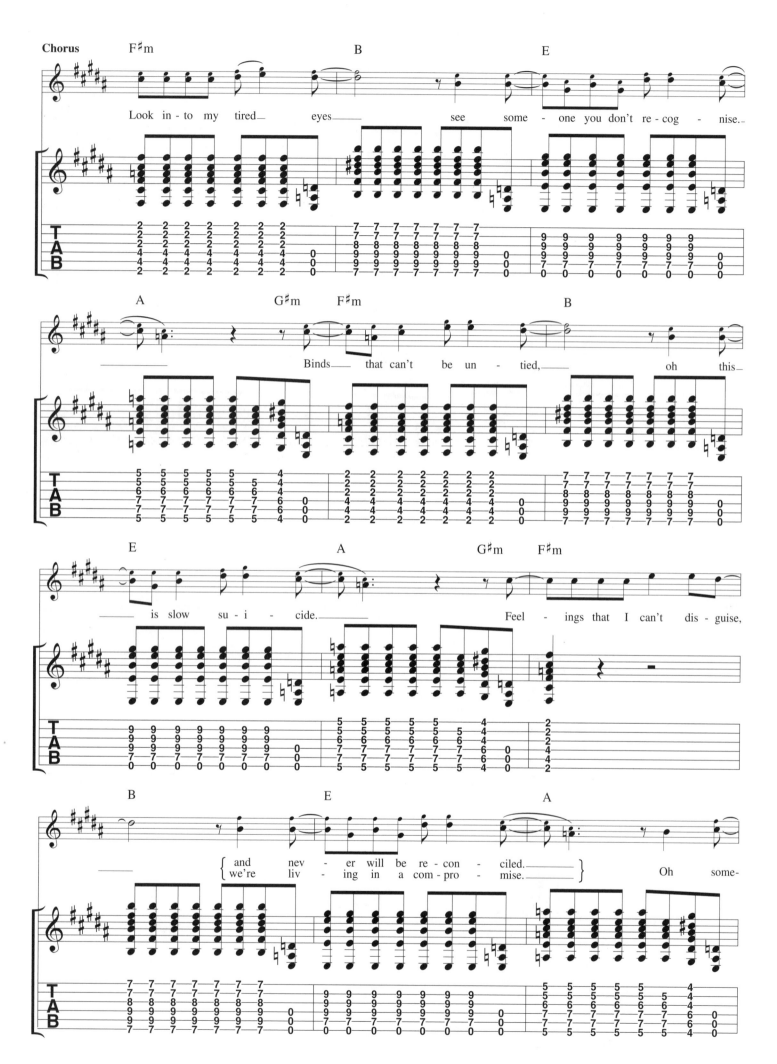

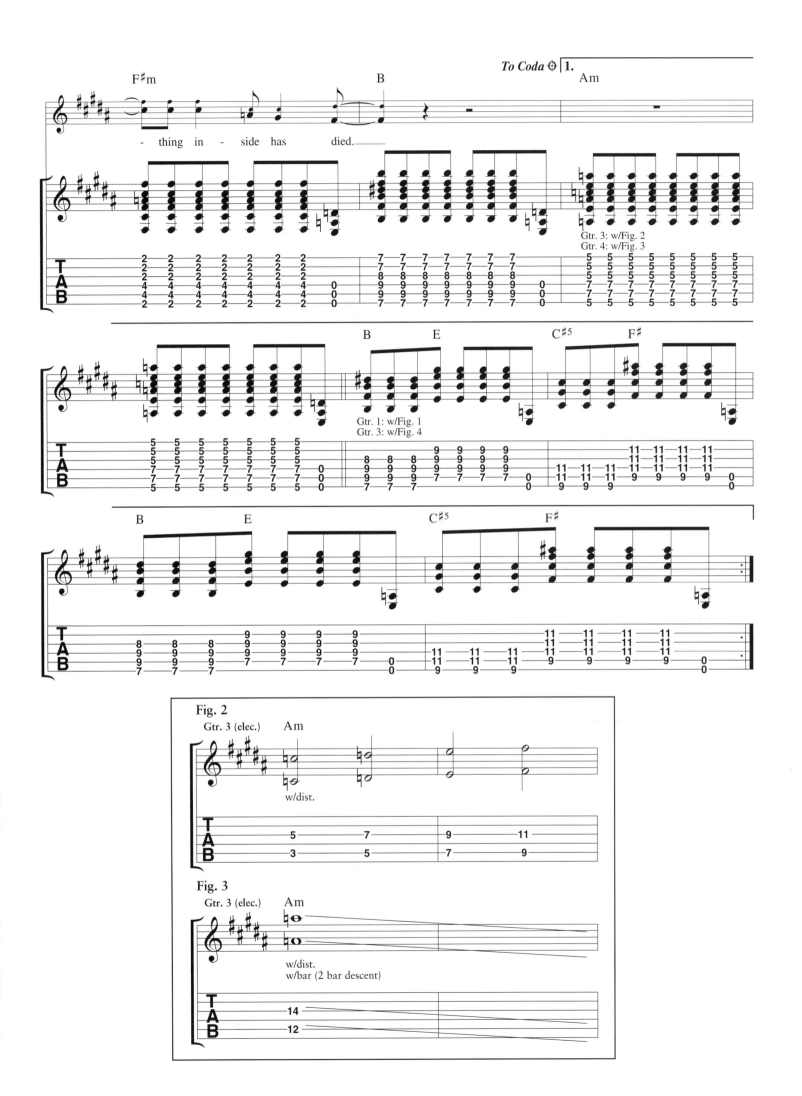

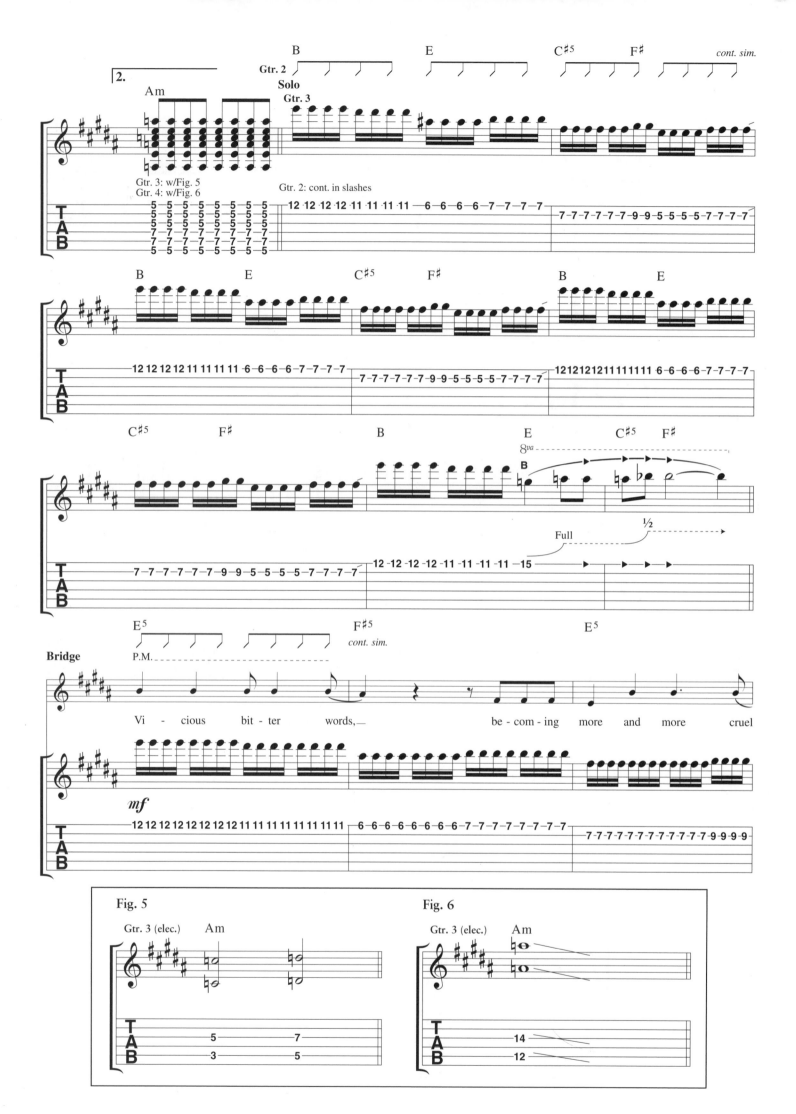

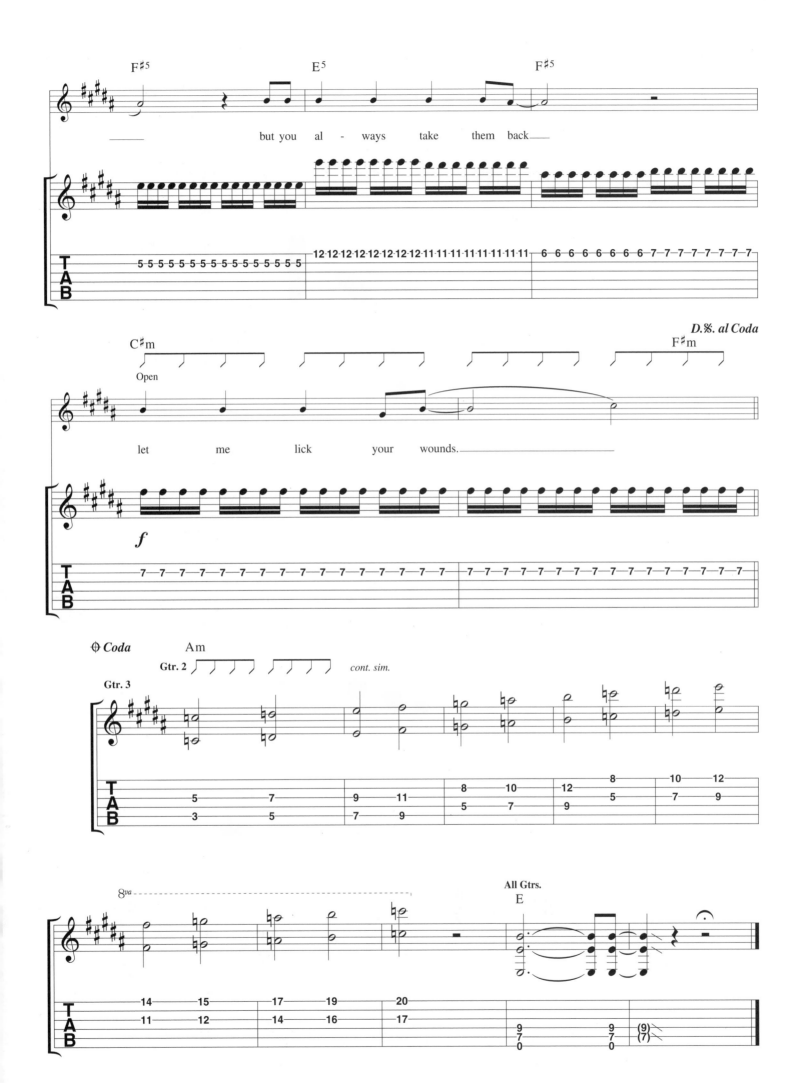

but you al - ways take them back

let me lick your wounds.

ENVY

WORDS & MUSIC BY TIM WHEELER

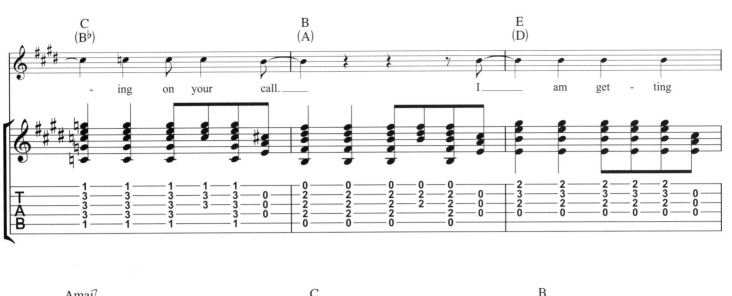

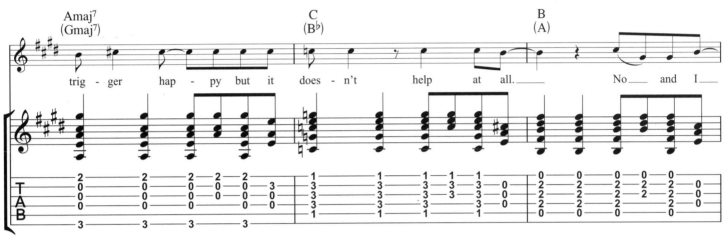

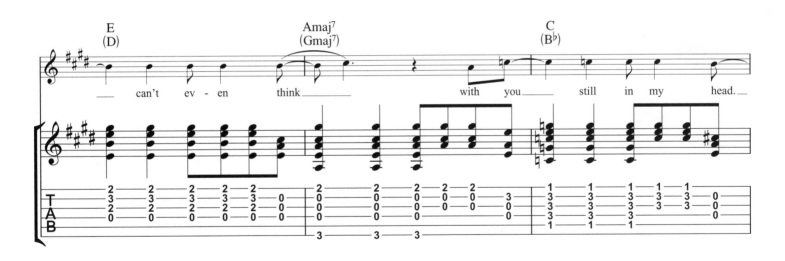

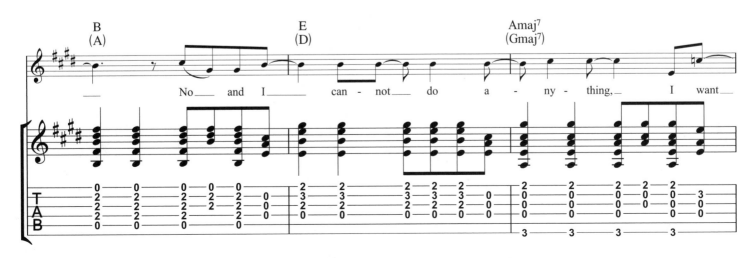

14

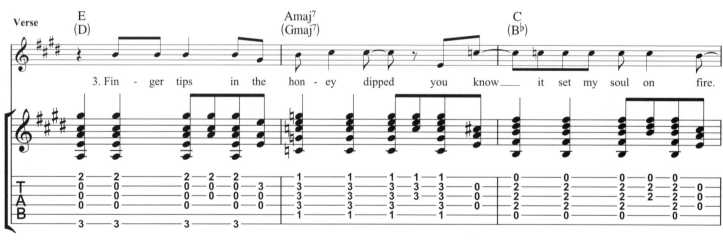

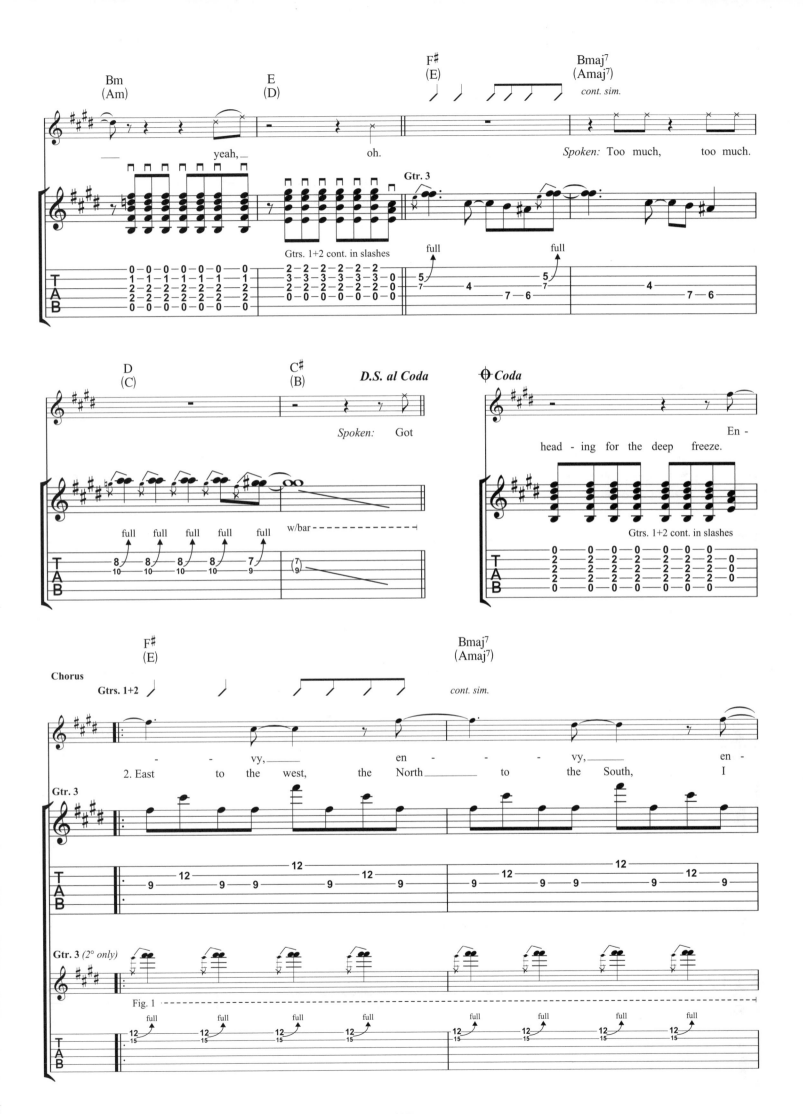

GIRL FROM MARS

WORDS & MUSIC BY TIM WHEELER

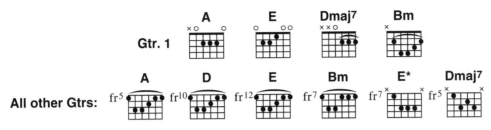

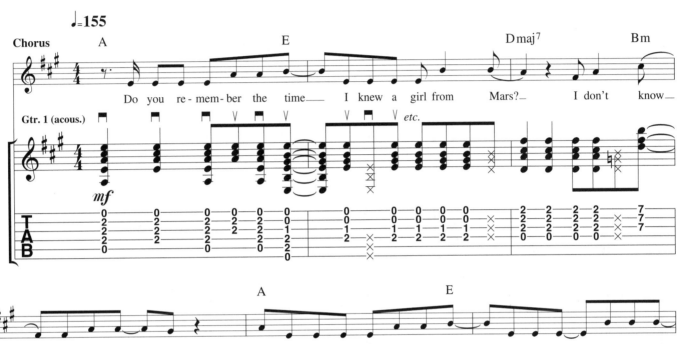

22

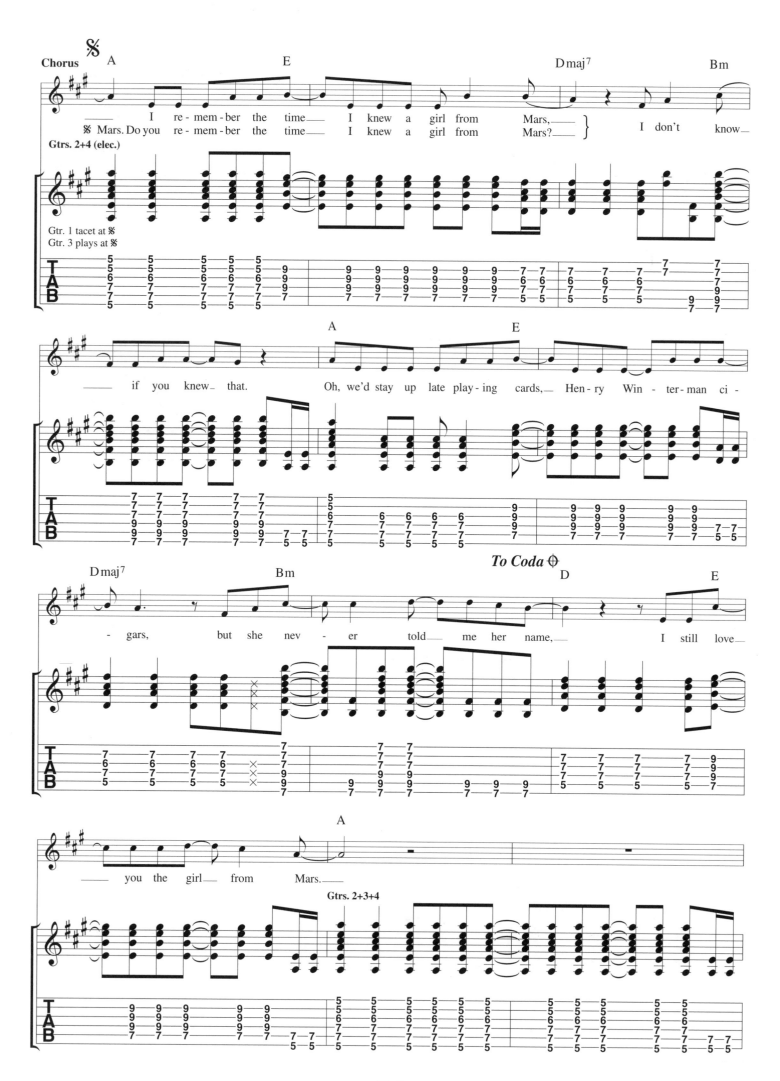

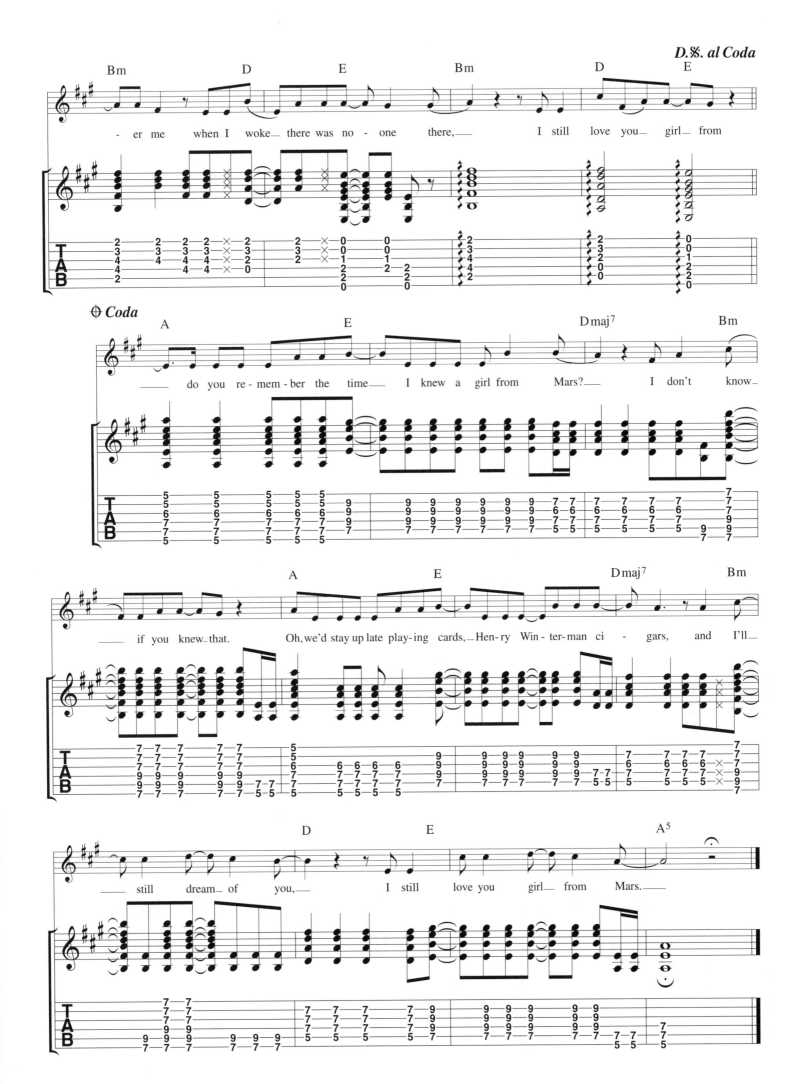

SHINING LIGHT

WORDS & MUSIC BY TIM WHEELER

These are the days you of - ten say,— there's no - thing that we can - not do.— Be - neath—
North star in the fir - ma - ment— you— shine the most bright.— I've seen—

— a ca - no - py— of stars, I'd— shed blood for you.—
— you draped in an e - lec - tric veil— shroud.

- ed in ce - les - ti - al light.—

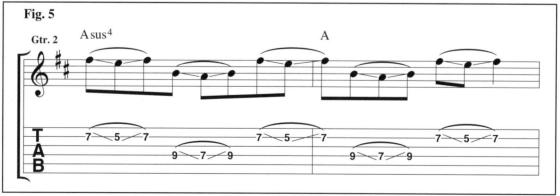

Fig. 5

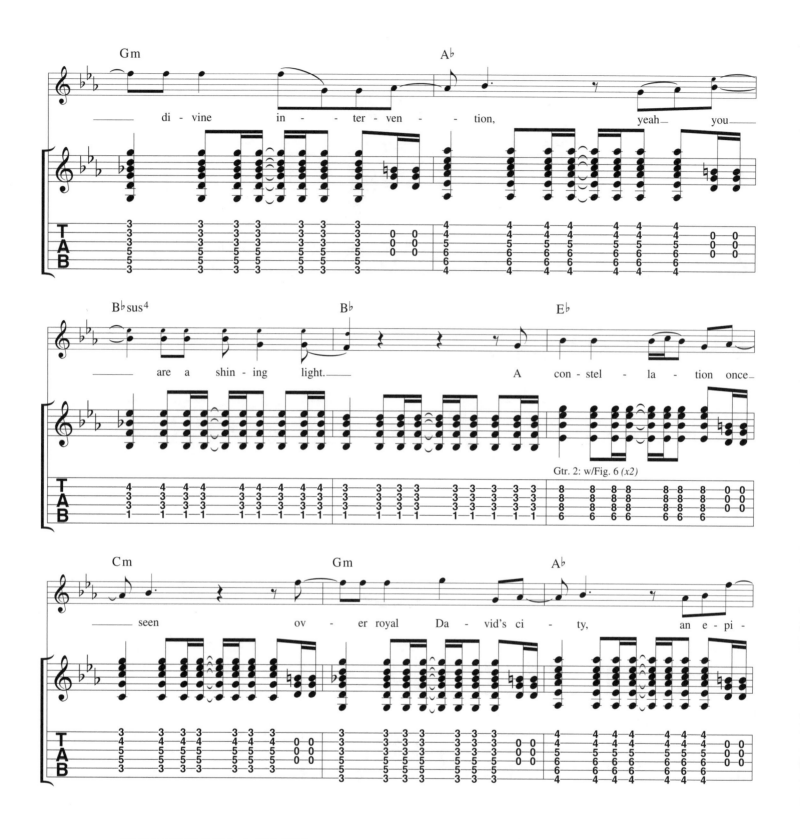

di - vine in - ter - ven - - tion,   yeah___ you___

B♭sus⁴   B♭   E♭

___ are a shin - ing light.___   A con - stel - la - tion once___

Gtr. 2: w/Fig. 6 (x2)

Cm   Gm   A♭

___ seen   ov - er royal Da - vid's ci - ty,   an e - pi -

Fig. 6

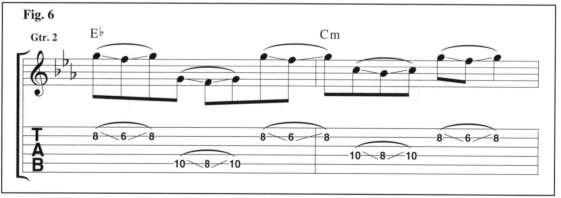

Gtr. 2   E♭   Cm

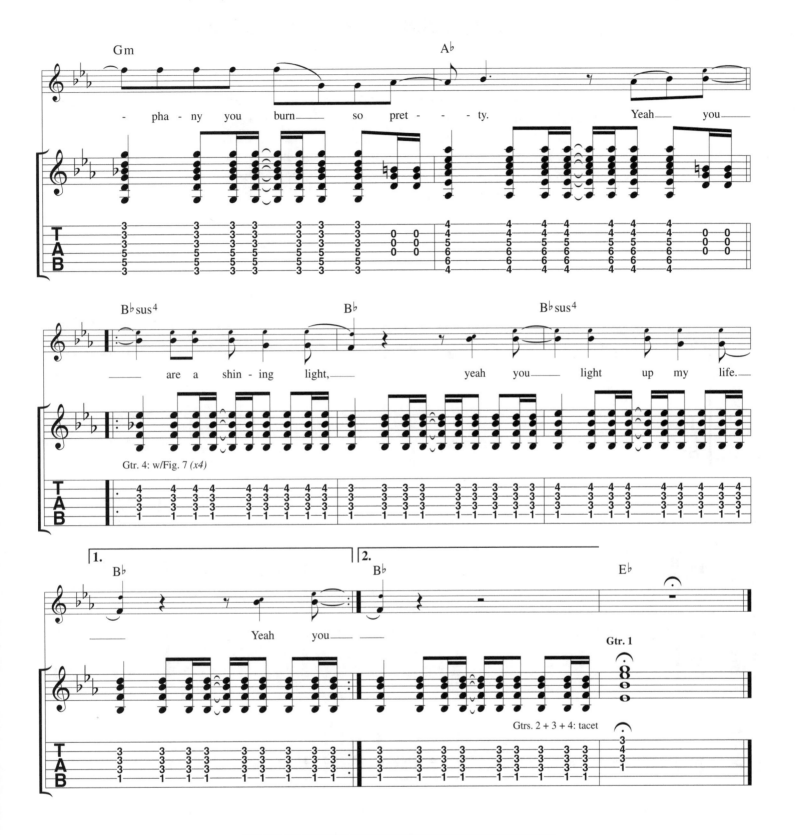

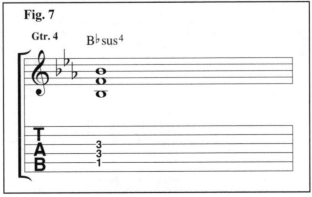

A LIFE LESS ORDINARY

WORDS & MUSIC BY TIM WHEELER

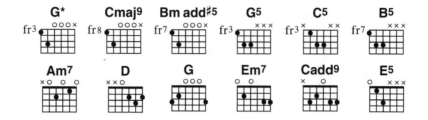

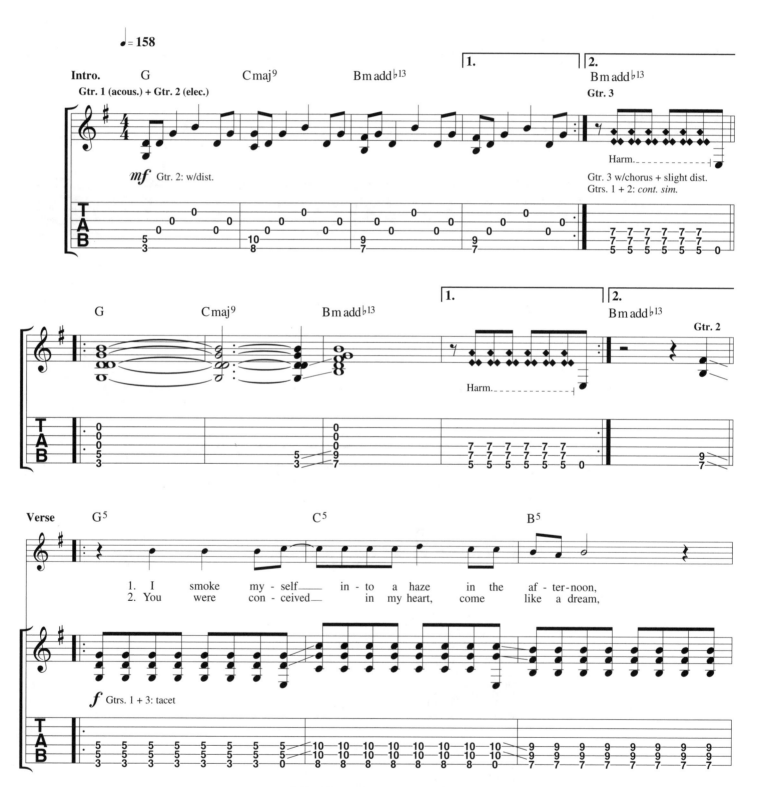

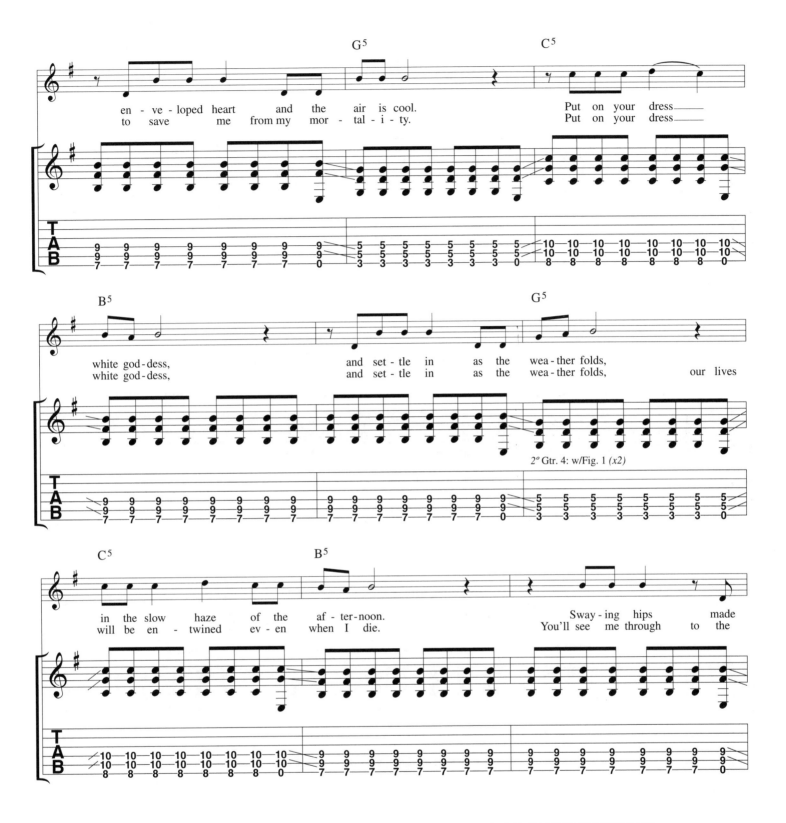

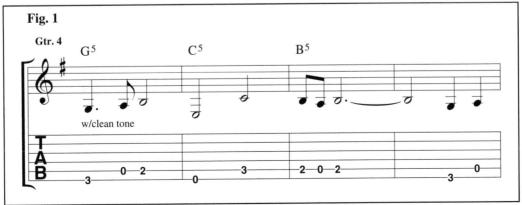

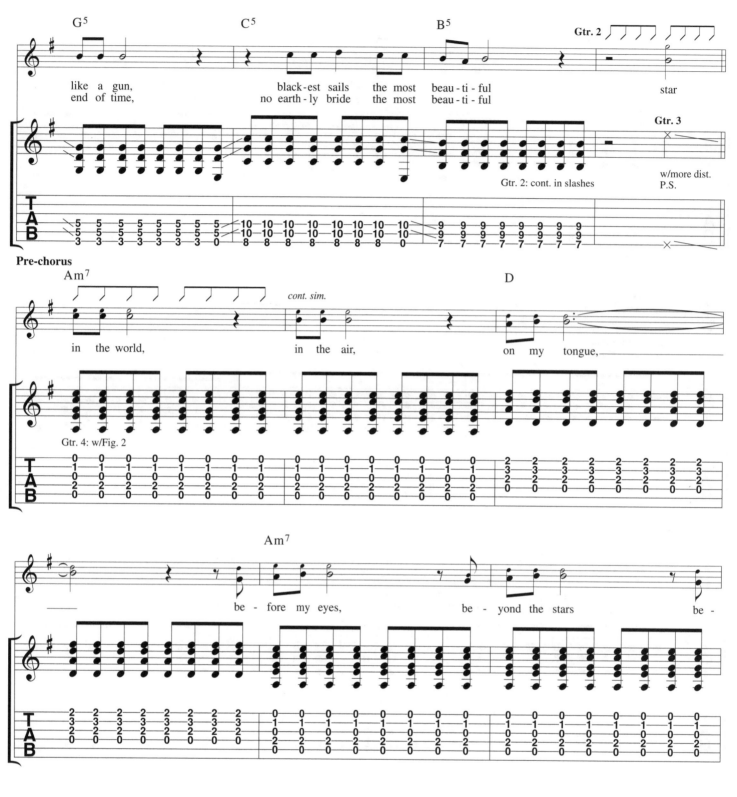

like a gun, black-est sails the most beau-ti-ful star
end of time, no earth-ly bride the most beau-ti-ful

Pre-chorus

in the world, in the air, on my tongue,—

be-fore my eyes, be-yond the stars be-

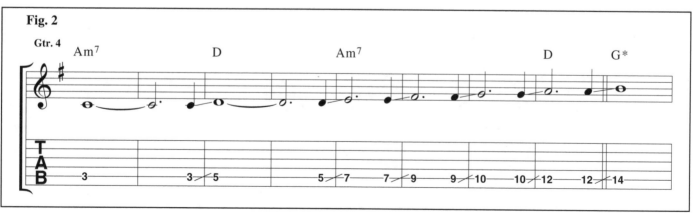

Fig. 2

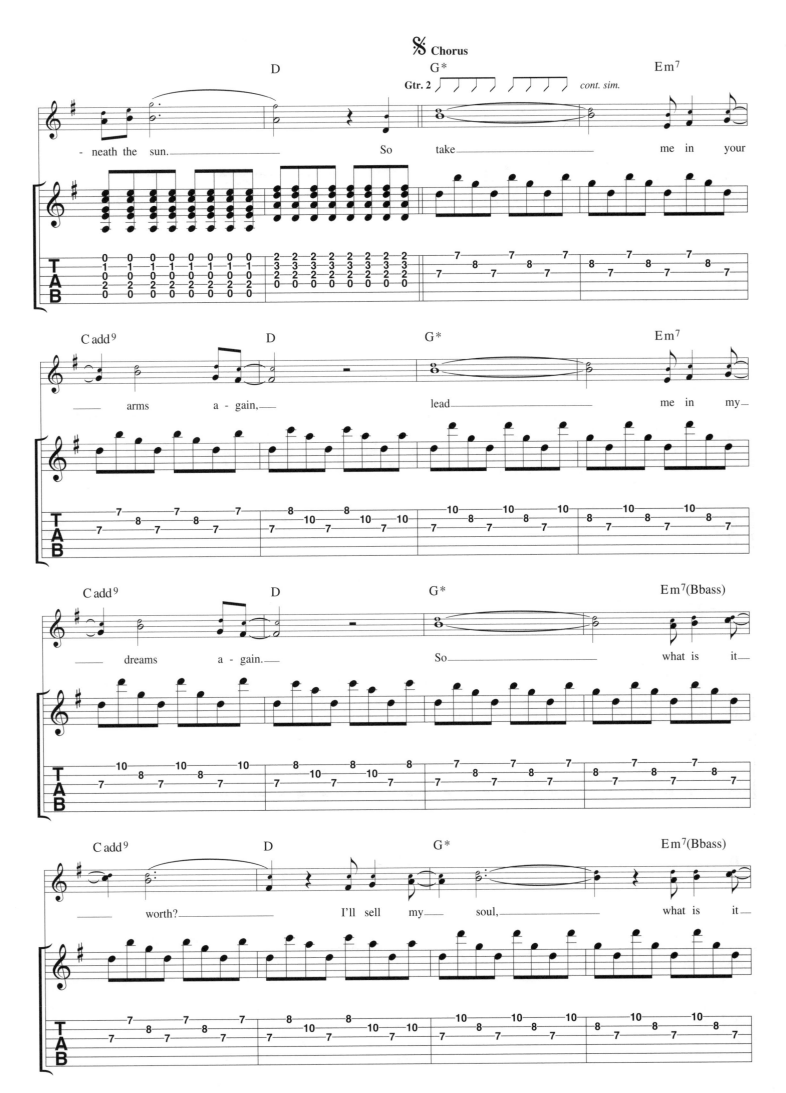

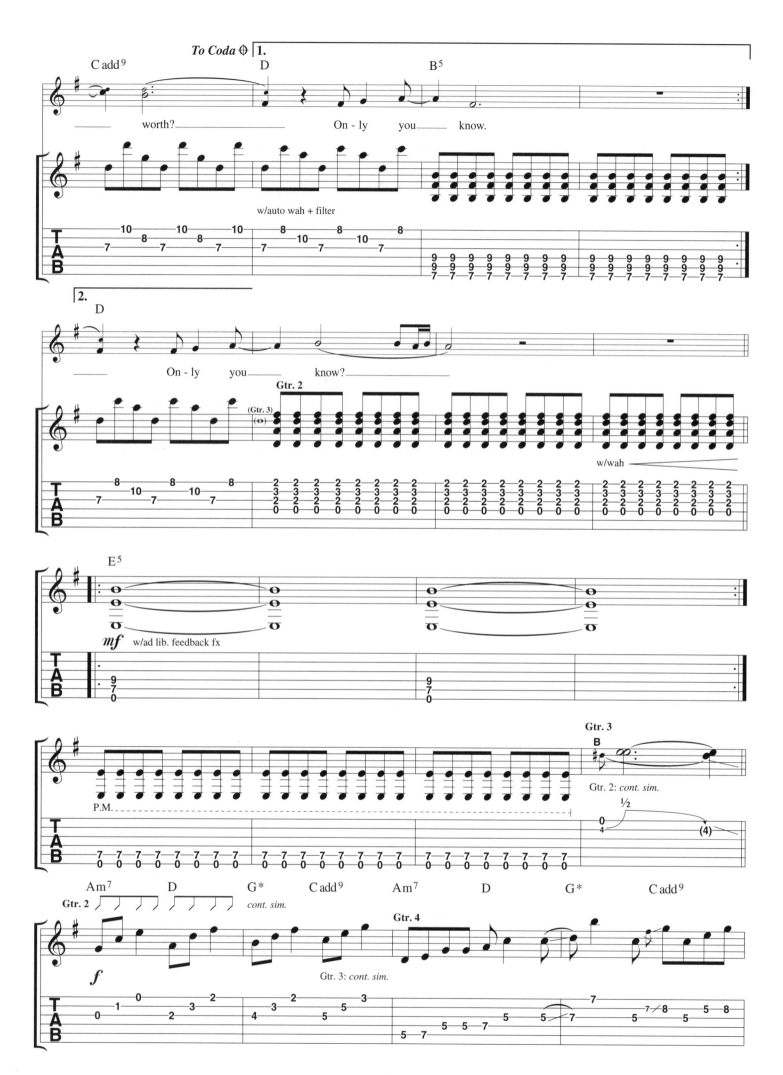

GOLDFINGER

WORDS & MUSIC BY TIM WHEELER

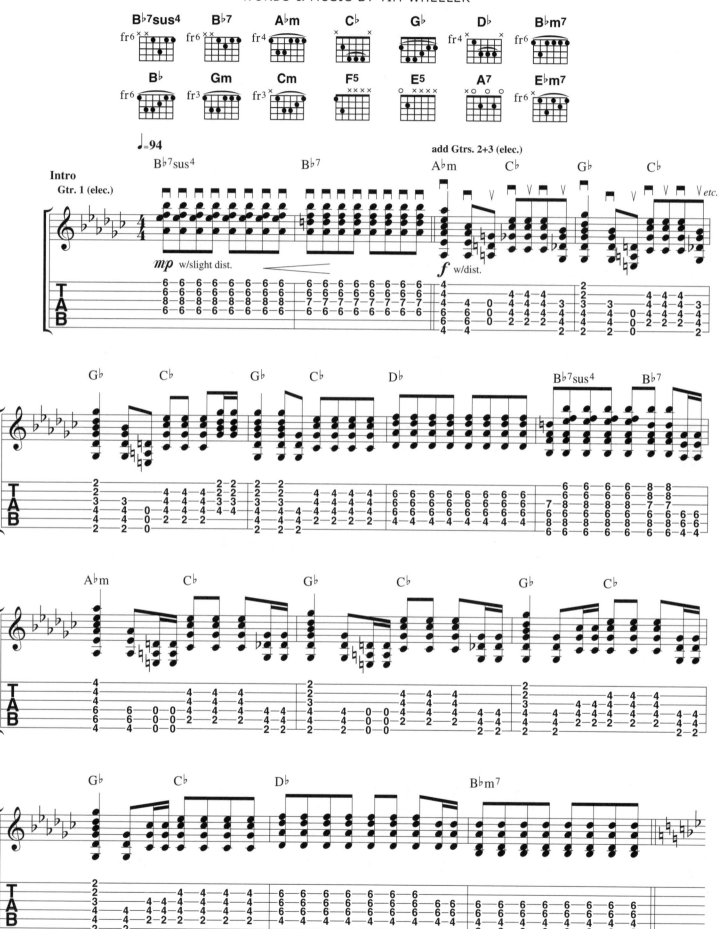

44

JESUS SAYS

WORDS BY TIM WHEELER
MUSIC BY MARK HAMILTON

Oo - oo - oh.___

Verse

1. One mill - ion light   years___ from home,___
(Verses 2–4 see block lyric)

Gtr. 3

4°, Gtr. 2 tacet (8 bars)

throw-ing   up   and feel - ing   small.___   Where   have   I   gone   and   land -

Outro

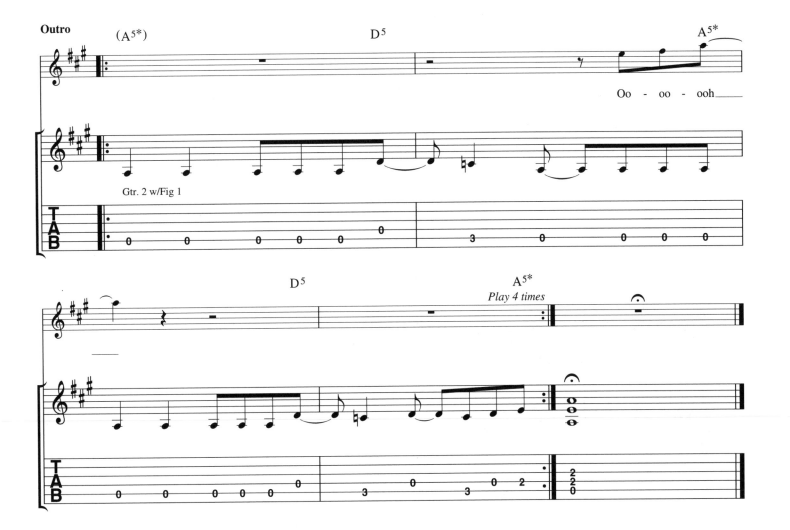

Oo - oo - ooh

Gtr. 2 w/Fig 1

Play 4 times

Verse 2:   Where have I gone and landed tonight
A million light years from home
Throwing up and feeling small
And now I know that my mind is blown.
'Cos there's something that I cannot live without
Something that I understand
Yeah, there's something that I cannot do without
And it's in your hand.

Verse 3:   Where have I gone and landed tonight
God give me strength
In a land of fakes and small time petty thieves
Must be the wrong place.
'Cos all my honesty is true, yeah
But it's gone to waste
On a soulless superficial void
Called the human race.

Verse 4:   Where have I gone and landed tonight
Throwing up and feeling small
One million light years from home
I've been shot right to the core
Of N. Y. C. and hostility, yeah!
But you gotta laugh
'Cos there's something that I cannot do without
And it's in your hand.

OH YEAH

WORDS & MUSIC BY TIM WHEELER

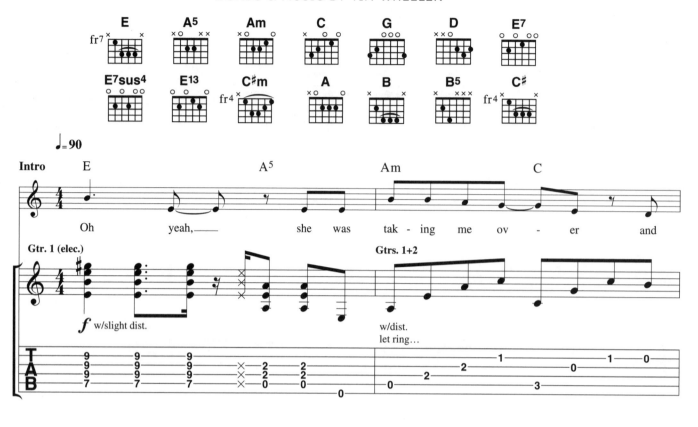

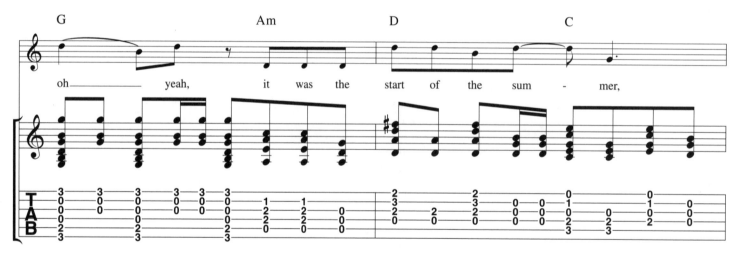

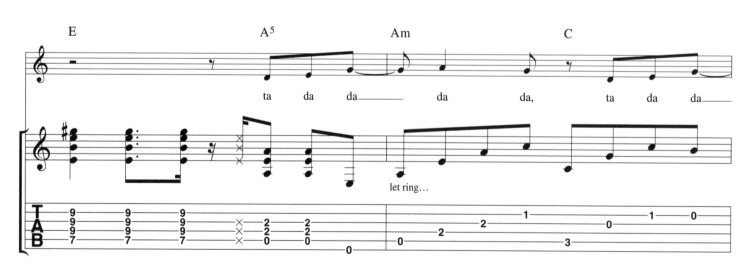

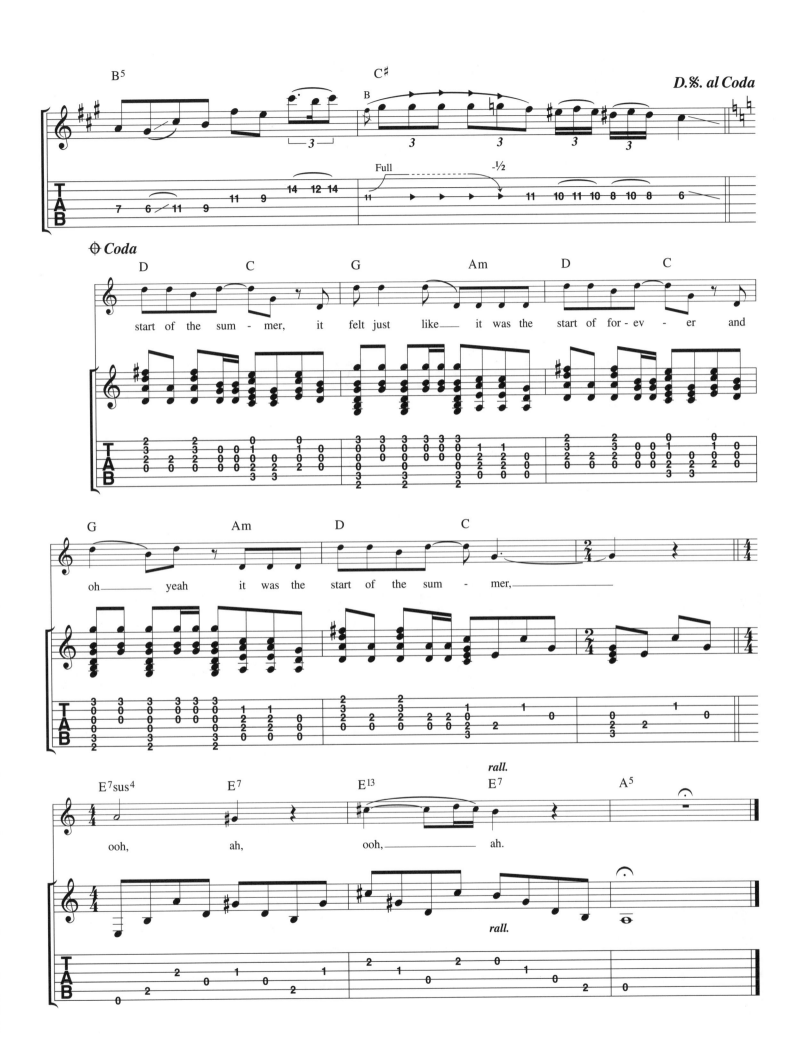

59

JACK NAMES THE PLANETS

WORDS & MUSIC BY TIM WHEELER

Verse 3:
I wish you'd come back everything's ready for you
You are welcome if you plan to
You come walking and you know where
You've got to understand that you got to care
I said I'd kiss you if you want
You've got things back to front
My mother's dying I've got to go home
But there's more you won't be solely on your own now.

SOMETIMES

WORDS & MUSIC BY TIM WHEELER

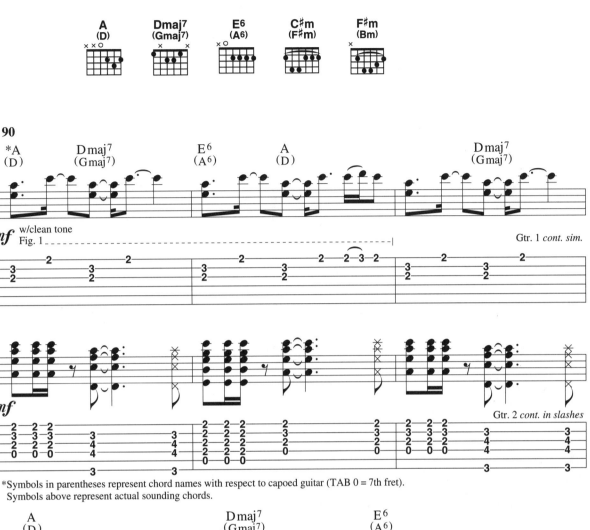

*Symbols in parentheses represent chord names with respect to capoed guitar (TAB 0 = 7th fret).
Symbols above represent actual sounding chords.

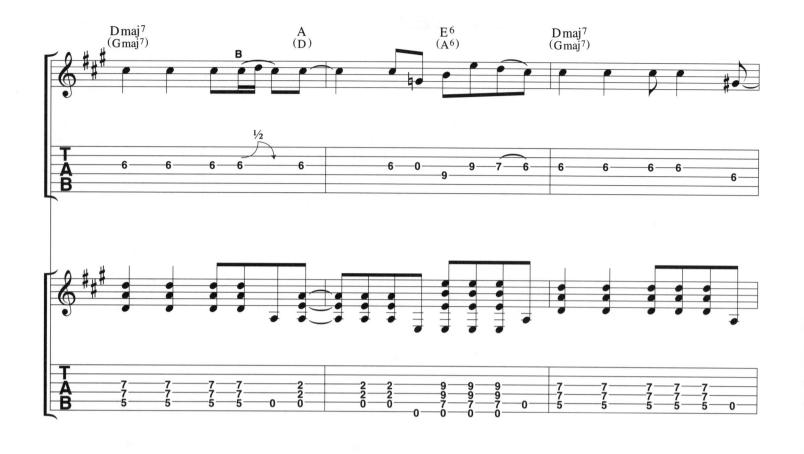

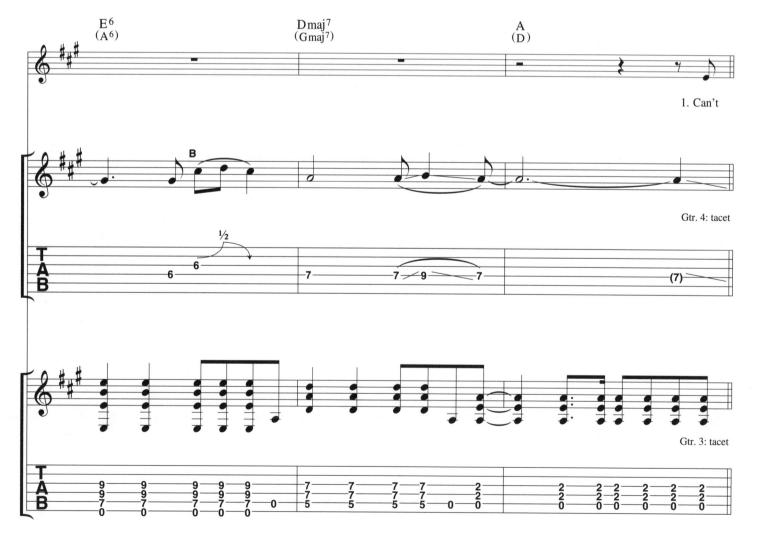

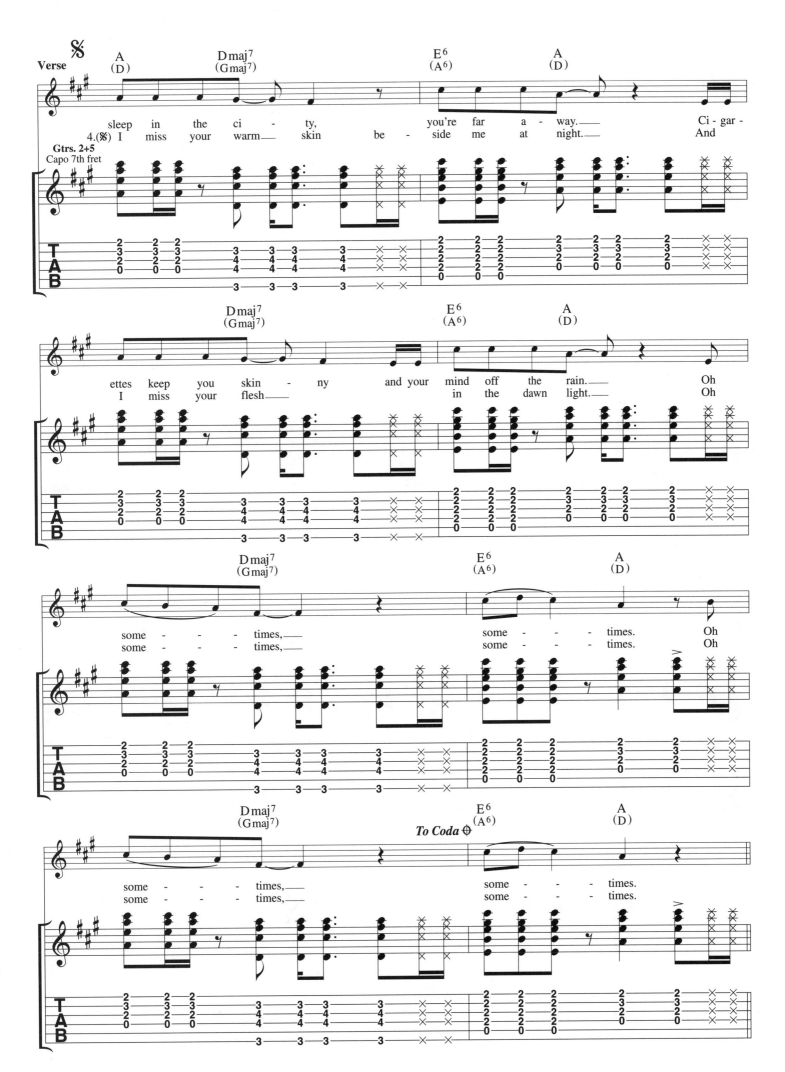

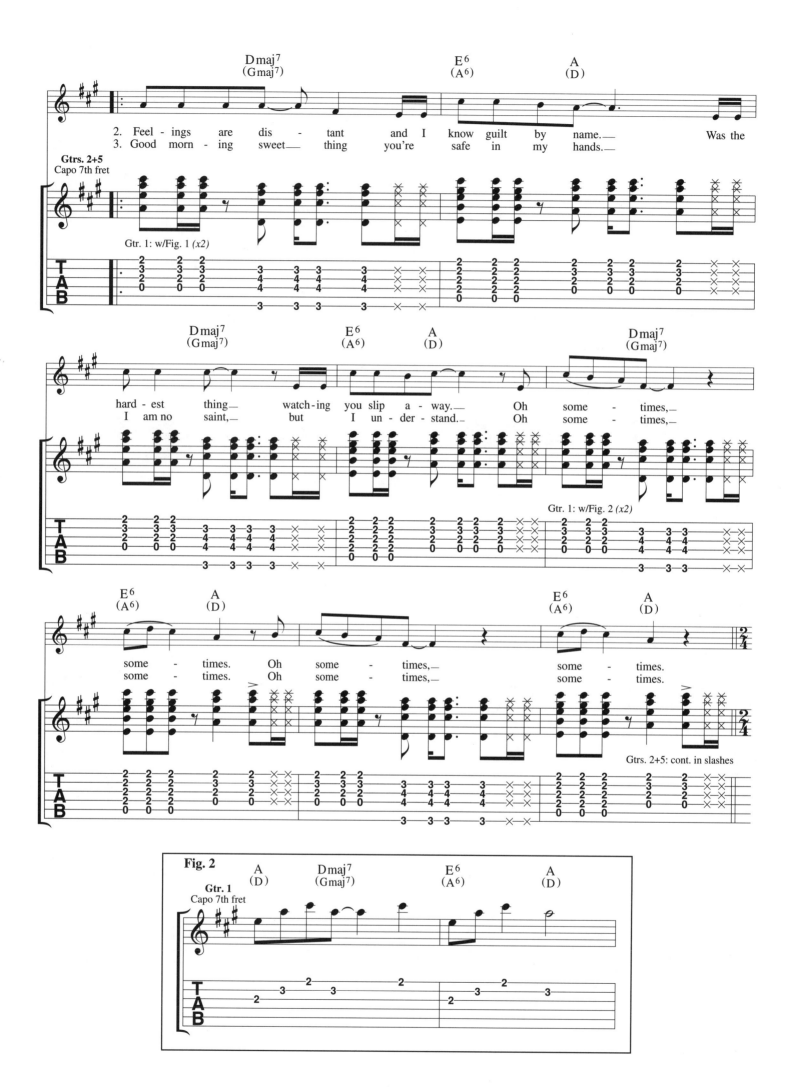

KUNG FU

WORDS & MUSIC BY TIM WHEELER

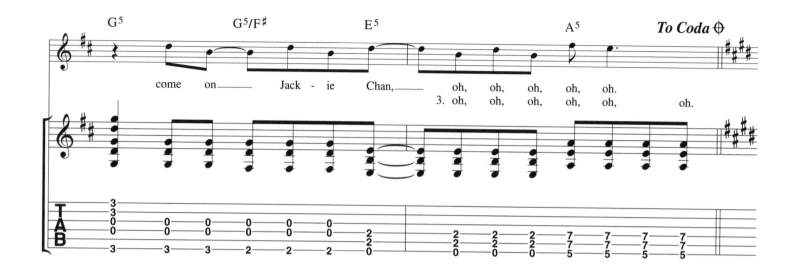

To Coda ⊕

come on —— Jack - ie Chan, —— oh, oh, oh, oh, oh.
3. oh, oh, oh, oh, oh, oh.

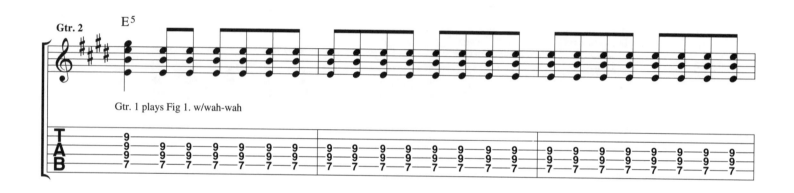

Gtr. 1 plays Fig 1. w/wah-wah

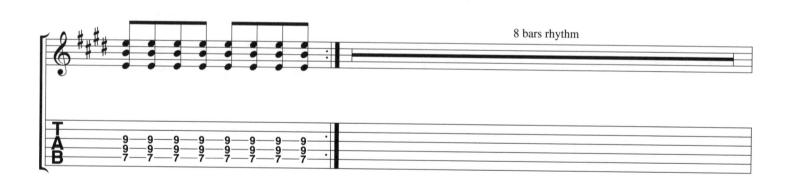

8 bars rhythm

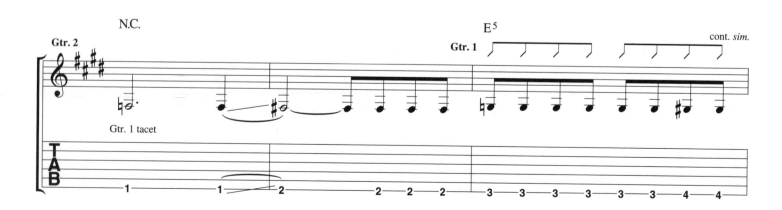

cont. *sim.*

Gtr. 1 tacet

CANDY

WORDS & MUSIC BY TIM WHEELER, BURT BACHARACH & HAL DAVID

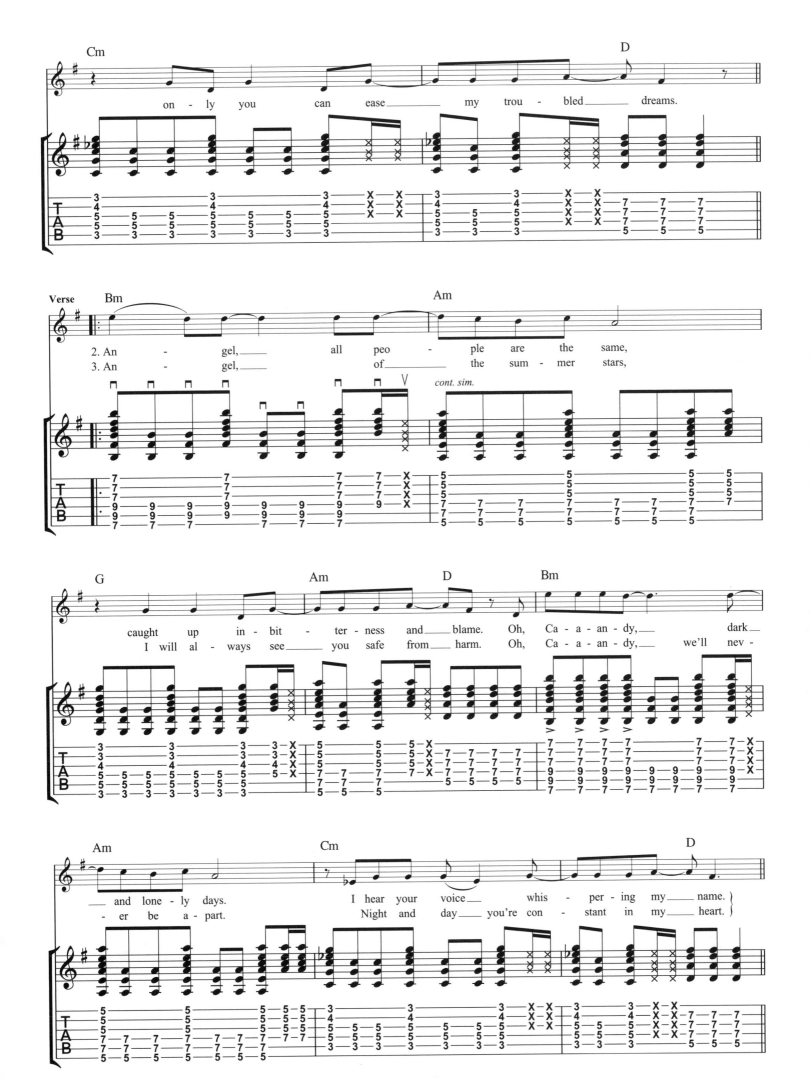

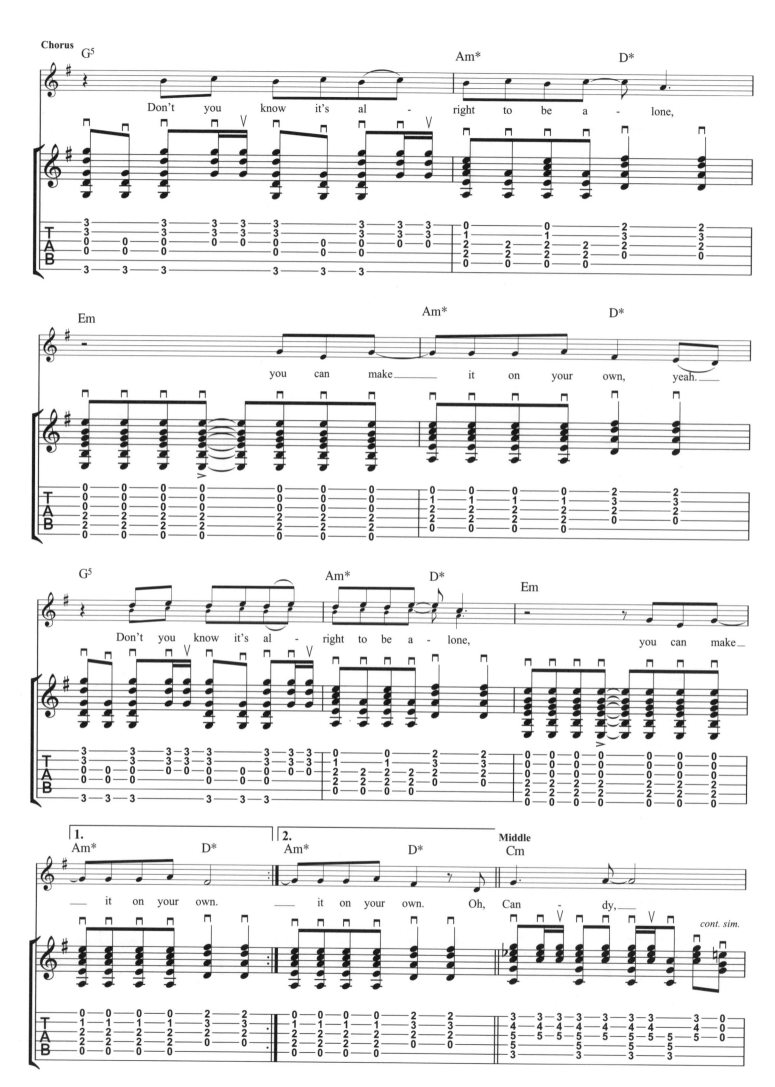

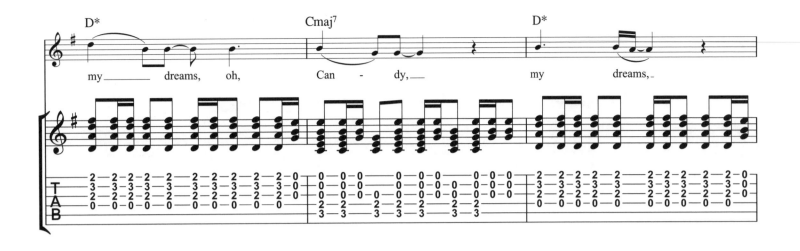

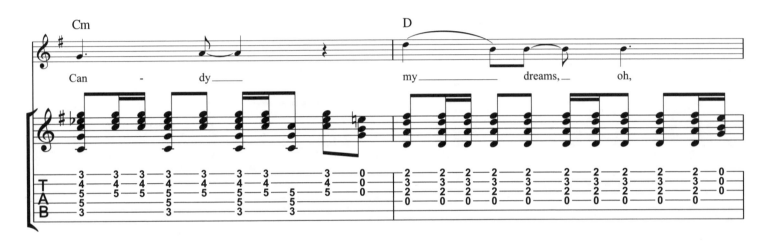

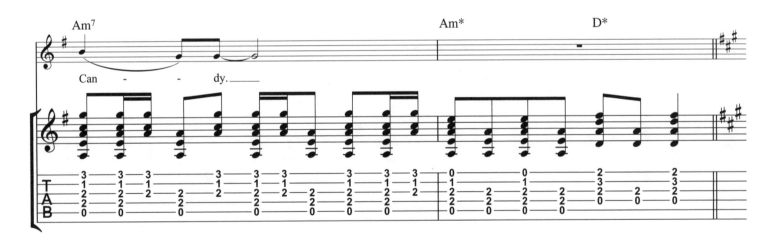

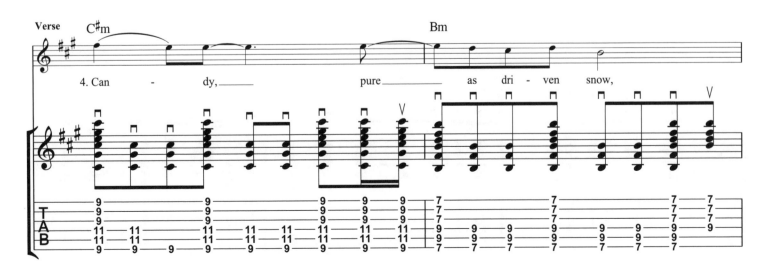

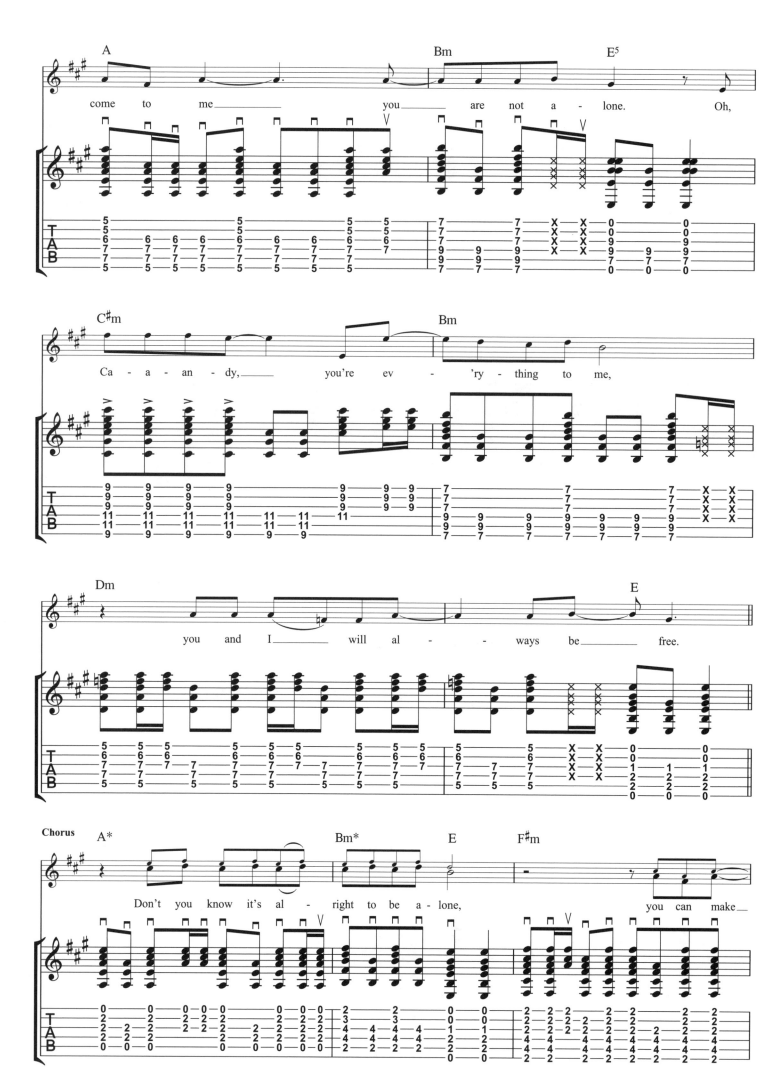

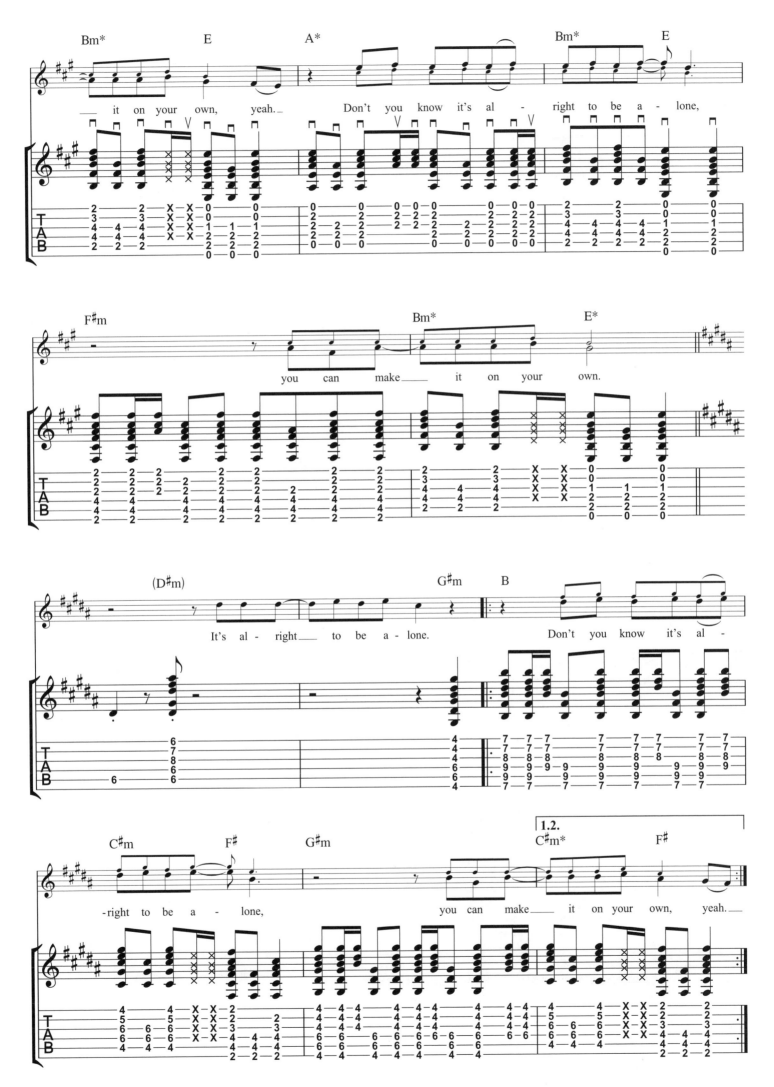

it on your own, yeah.

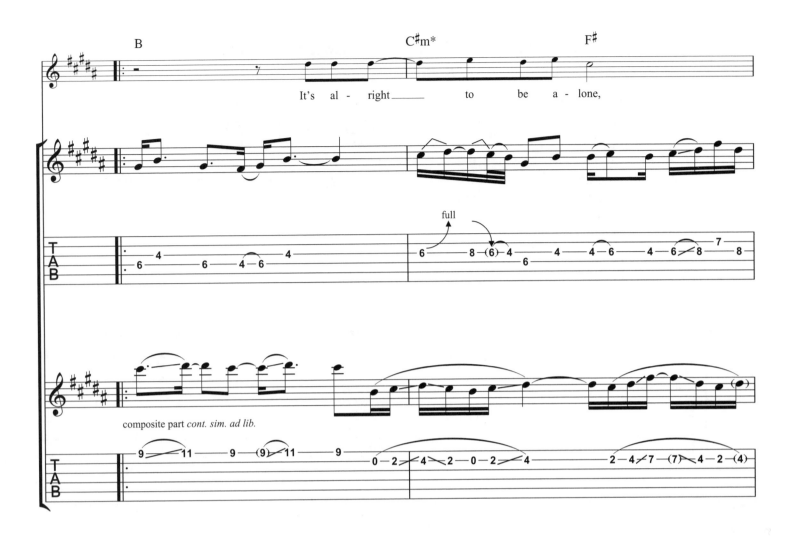

It's al - right___ to be a - lone,

composite part *cont. sim. ad lib.*

you can make___ it on your own, yeah.___

Repeat to fade

ANGEL INTERCEPTOR

WORDS & MUSIC BY TIM WHEELER & RICK MCMURRAY

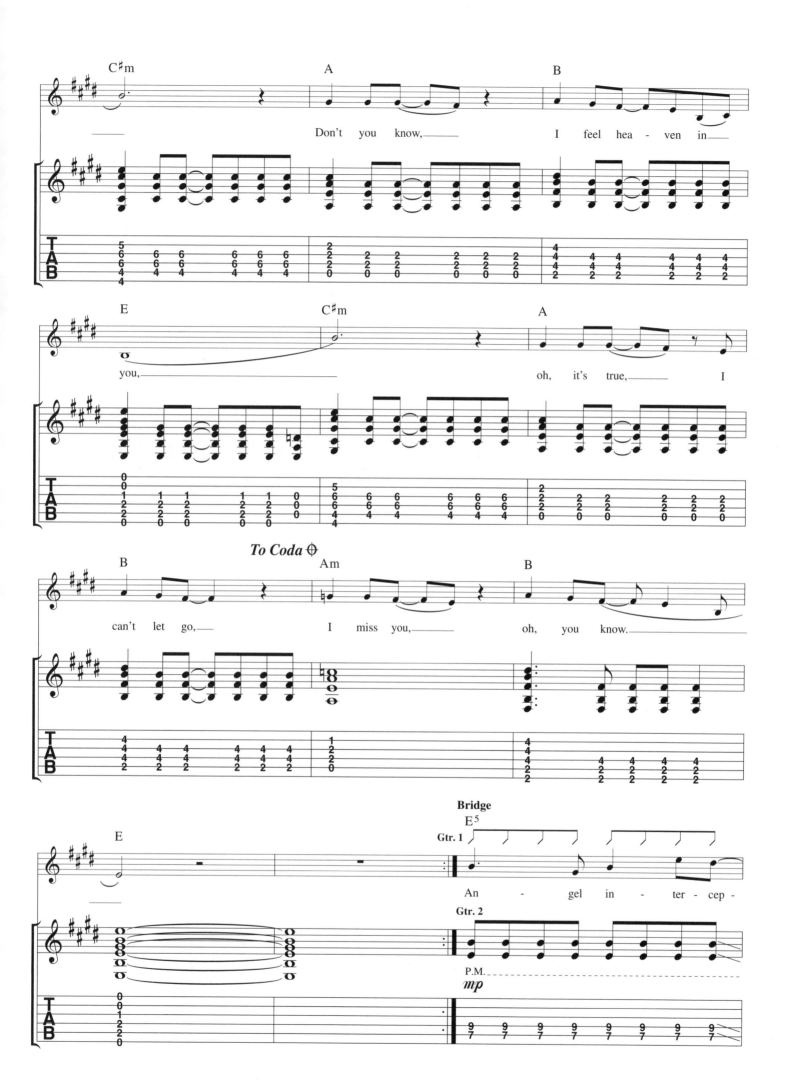

89

UNCLE PAT

WORDS & MUSIC BY TIM WHEELER

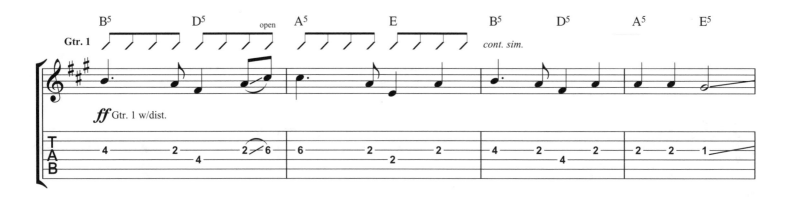

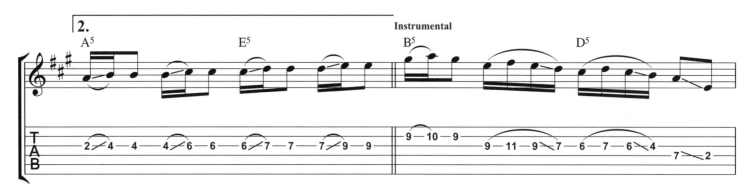

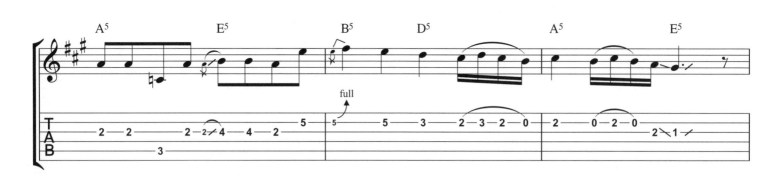

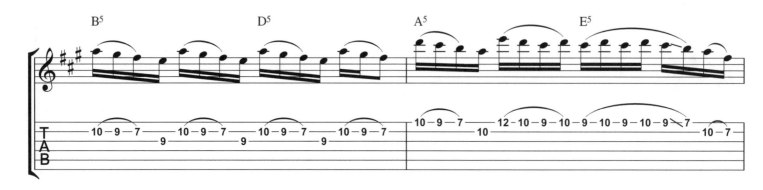

Verse 3:
At dusk I will make my way
Along the lanes and through the fields
To where my cottage is
But before I step inside for bed
I'll look up at the stars as we had
All these years ago.

WALKING BAREFOOT

WORDS & MUSIC BY TIM WHEELER

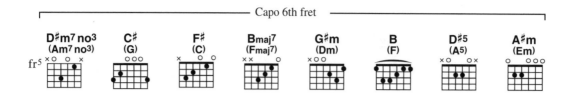

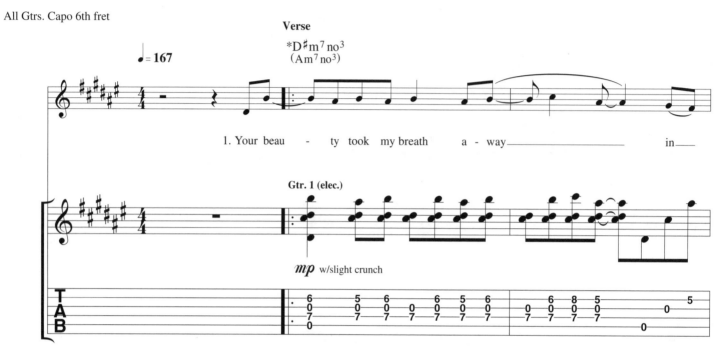

*Symbols in parentheses represent chord names with respect to capoed guitar (TAB 0 = 6th fret). Symbols above represent actual sounding chords.

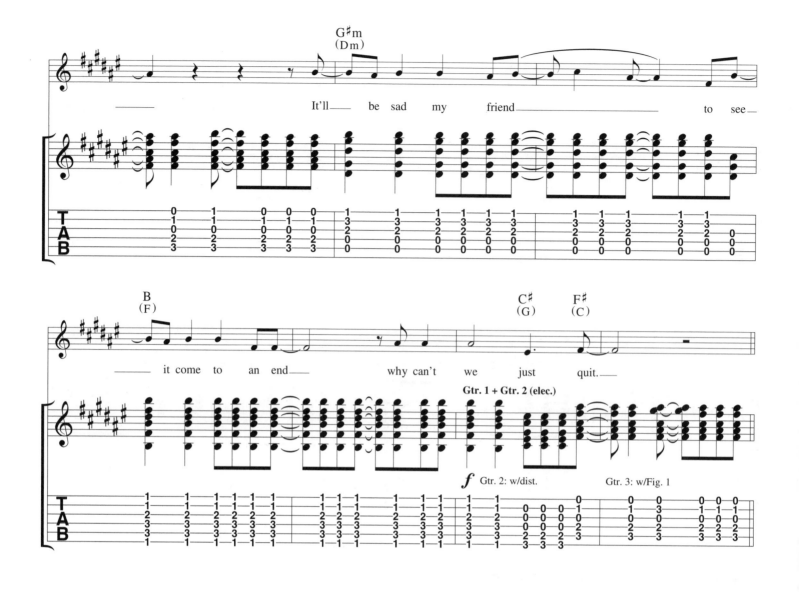

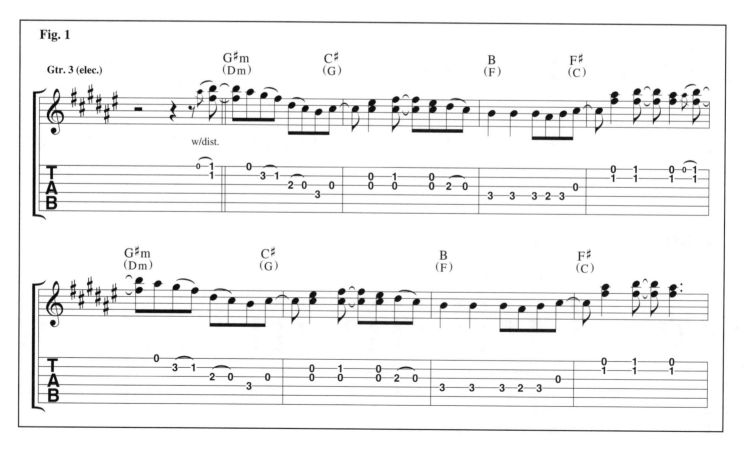

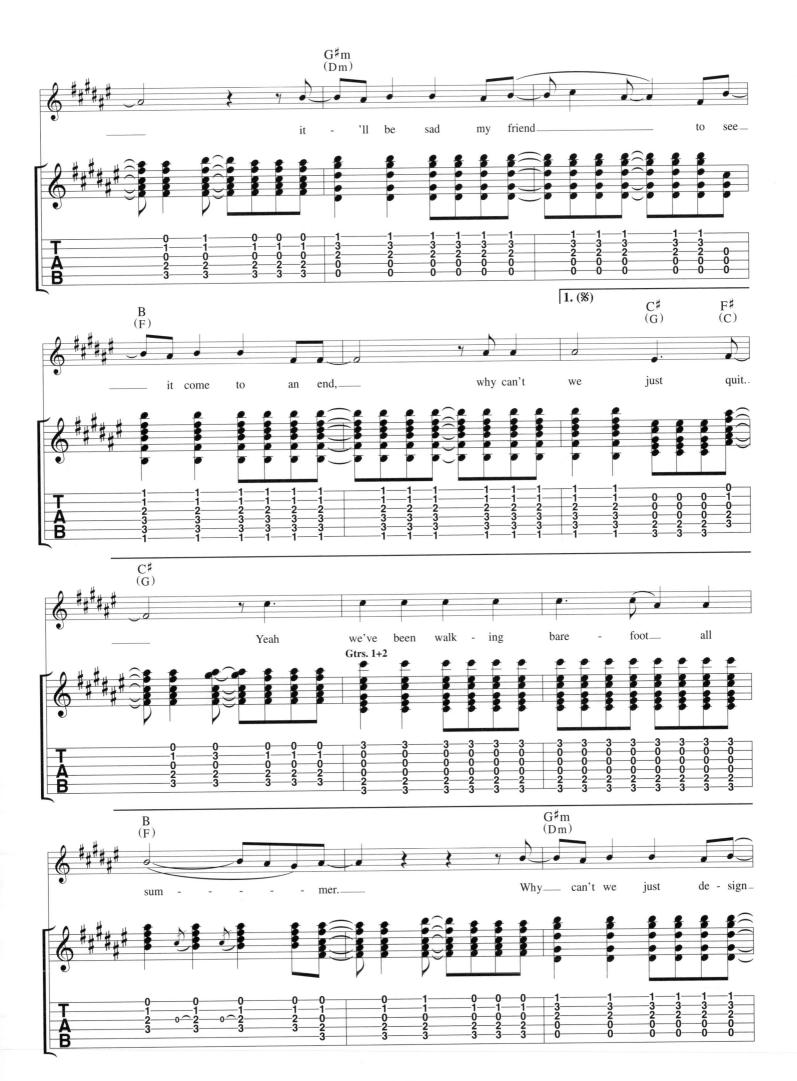

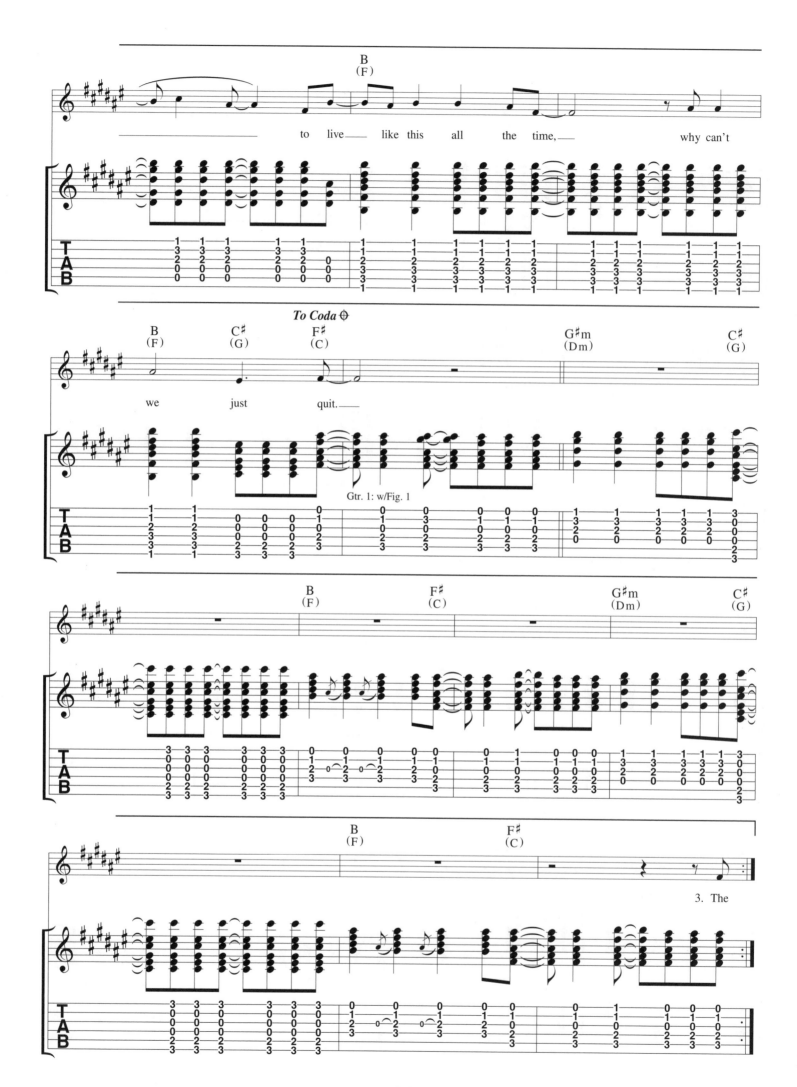

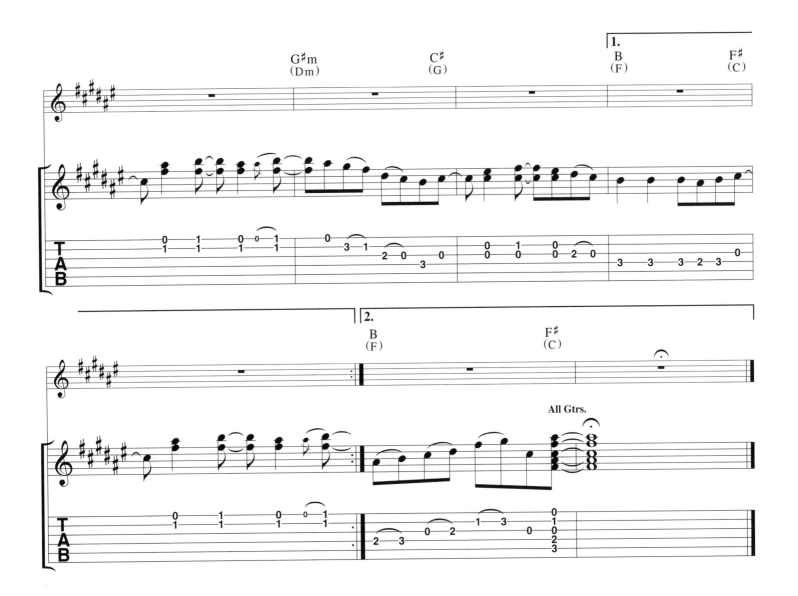

Verse 4:
When the summer's gone and the room is cold
When you're looking at the rain and it just won't go.
Remember when the sun was high up above
Remember when the days were long and we were in love.

Yeah we've been walking barefoot *etc.*

PETROL

WORDS BY TIM WHEELER
MUSIC BY MARK HAMILTON

Instrumental

Verse 3:
I've been preparing for days
I know exactly what to say
"No one will be around
No one will take me down"
They'll all get back in the cars
And maybe they'll go home
But the things they'll never know
Like where it is I go.

WILDSURF

WORDS & MUSIC BY TIM WHEELER & CHARLOTTE HATHERLEY

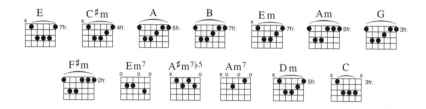

Come ___ on, ___ yeah, come on while we still ___ can, ___

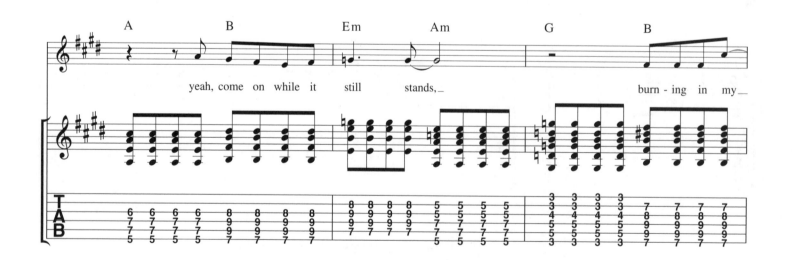

yeah, come on while it still ___ stands, ___ burn - ing in my ___

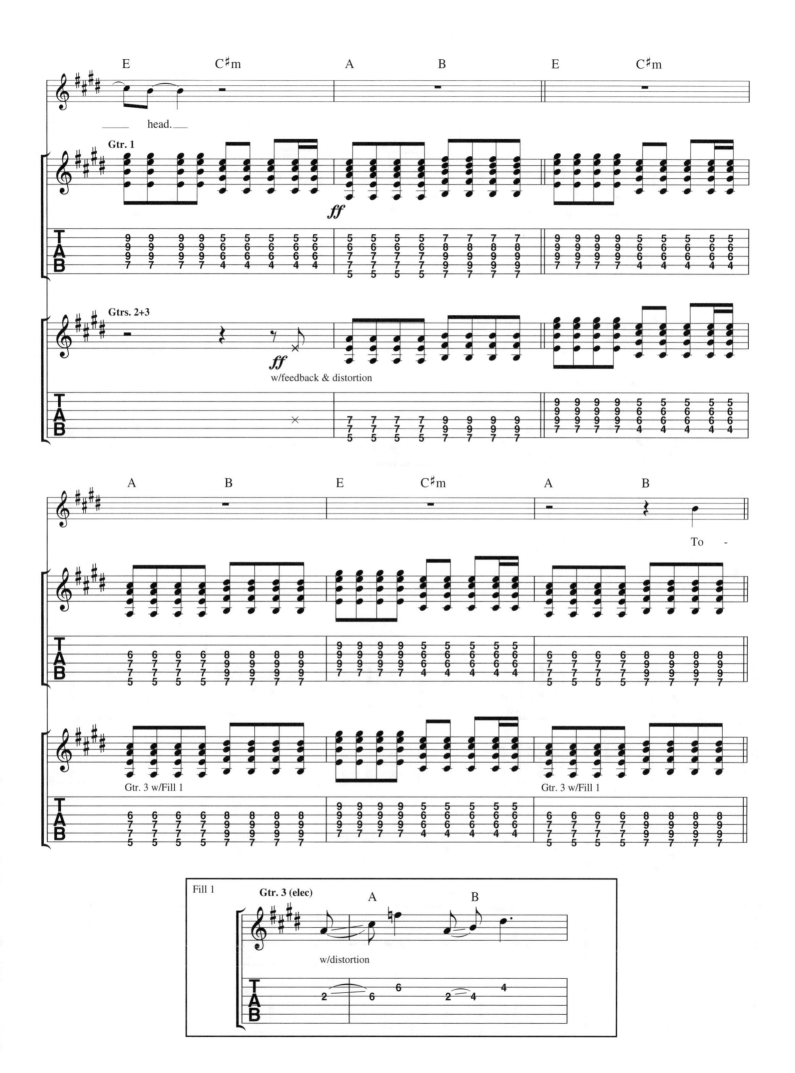

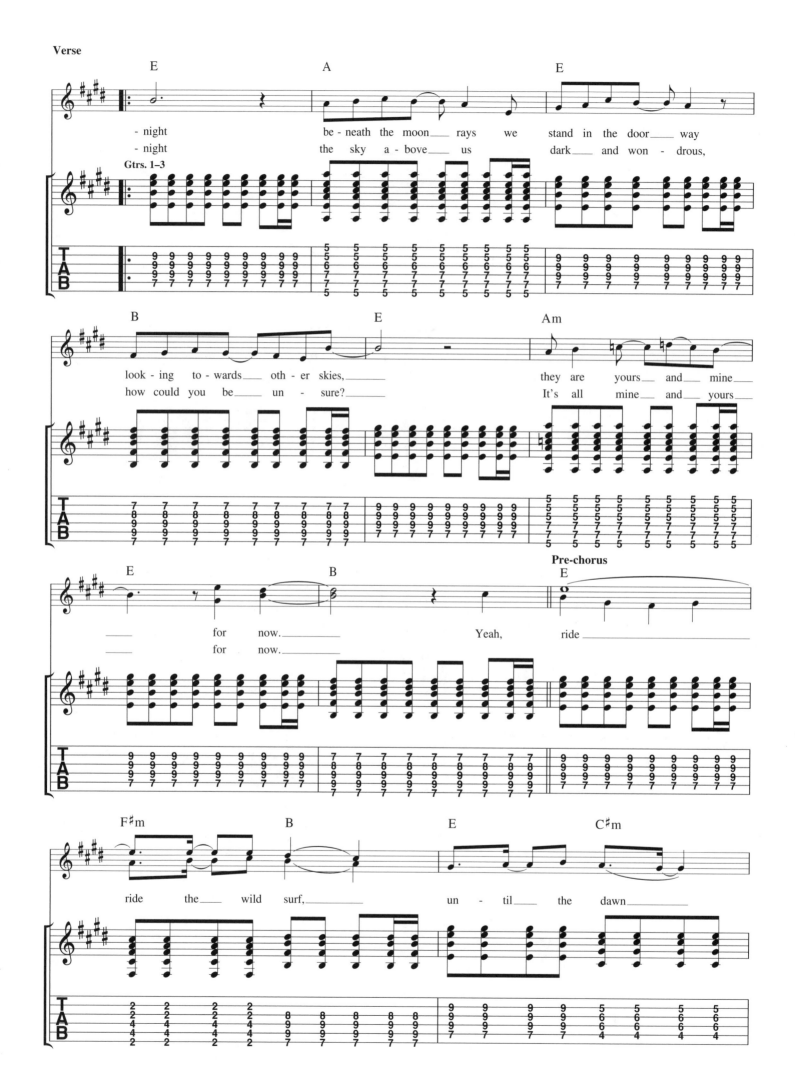

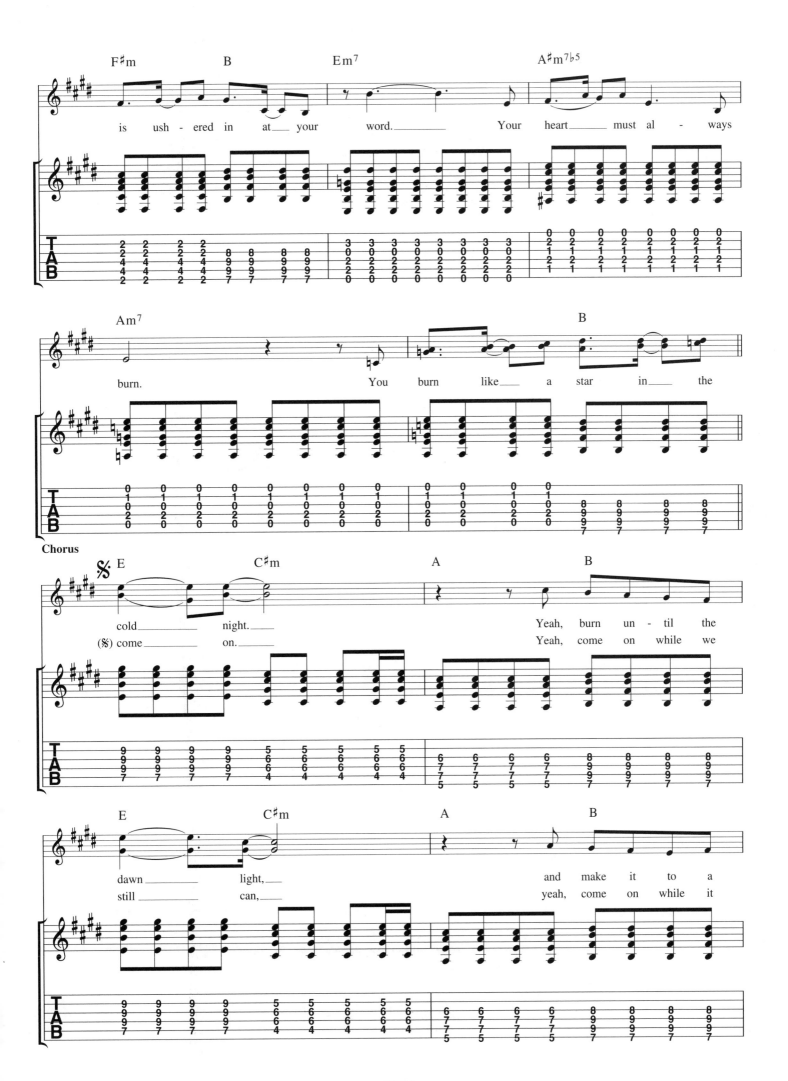

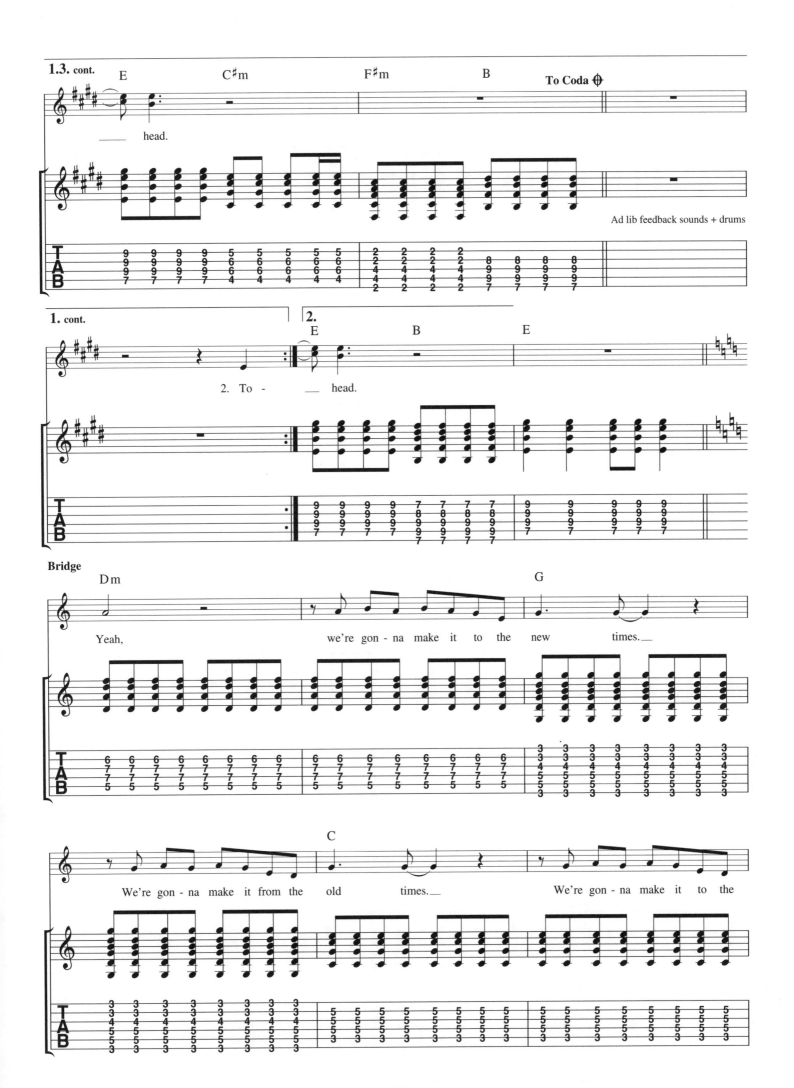

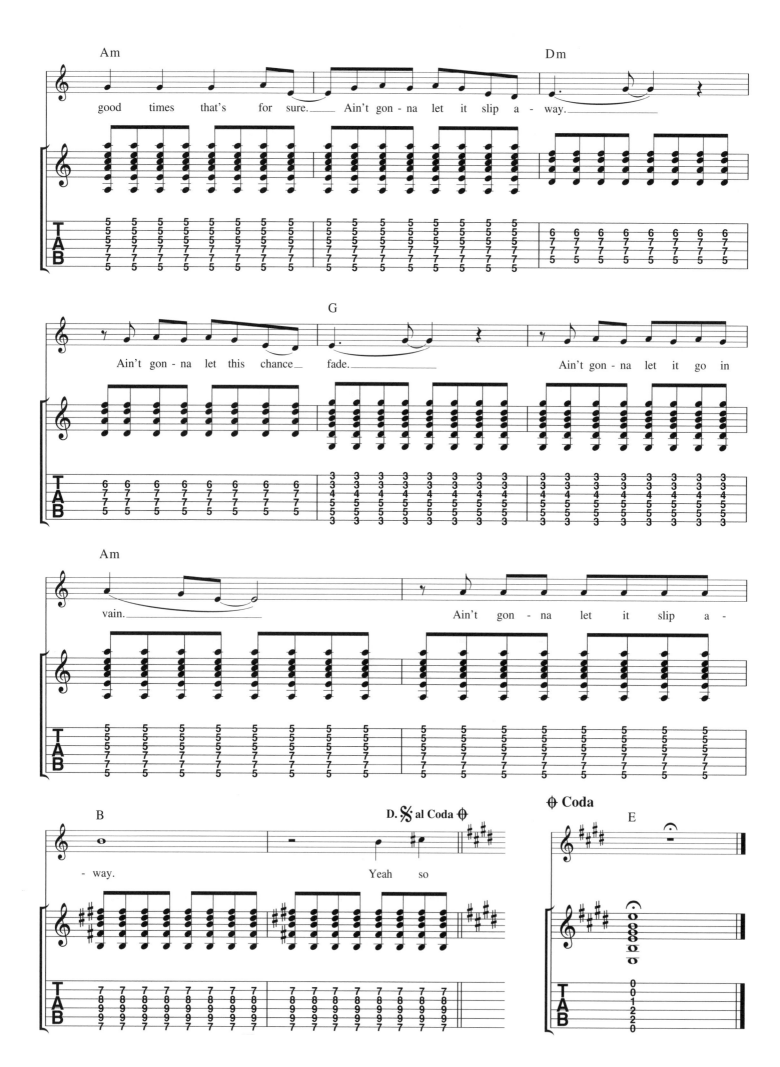

THERE'S A STAR

WORDS & MUSIC BY TIM WHEELER

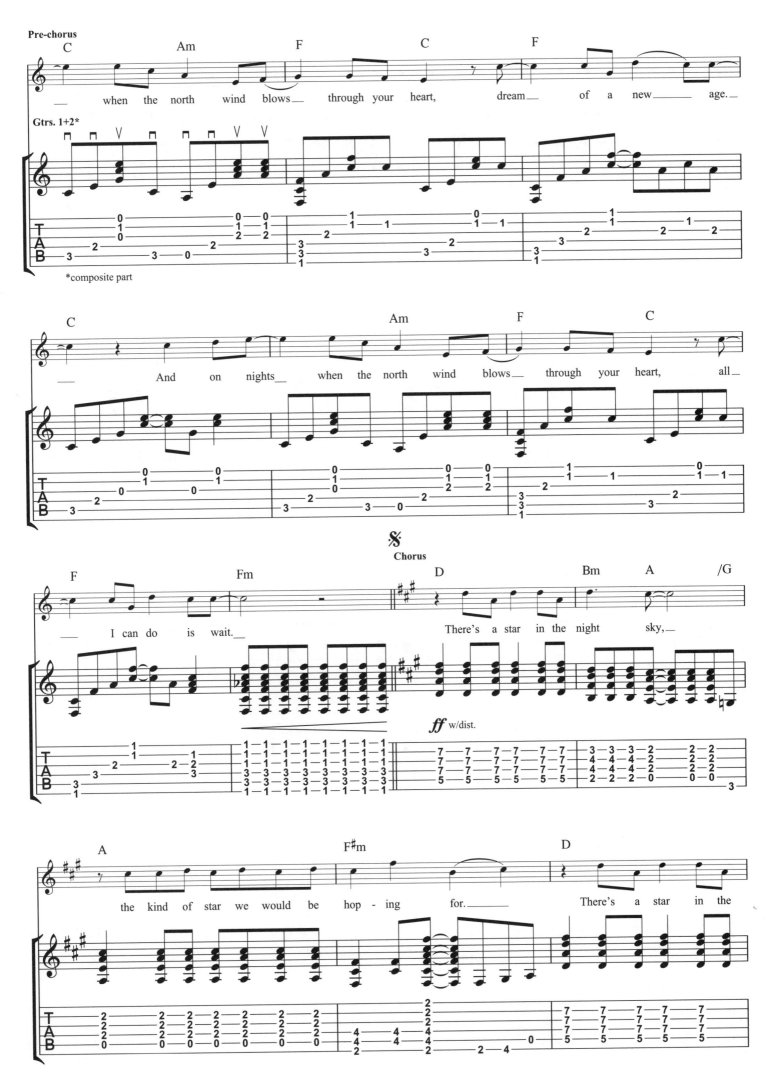

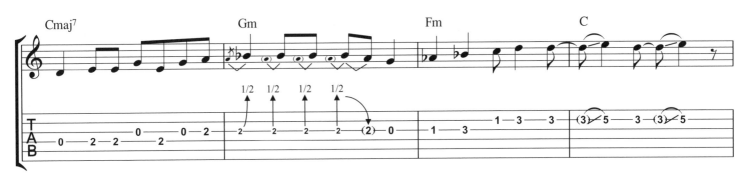

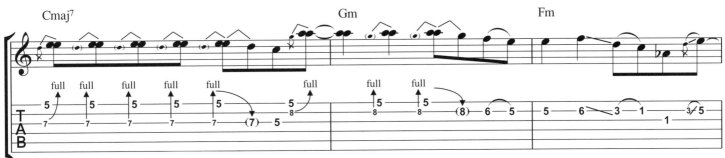

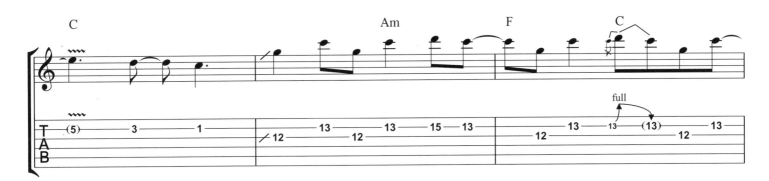

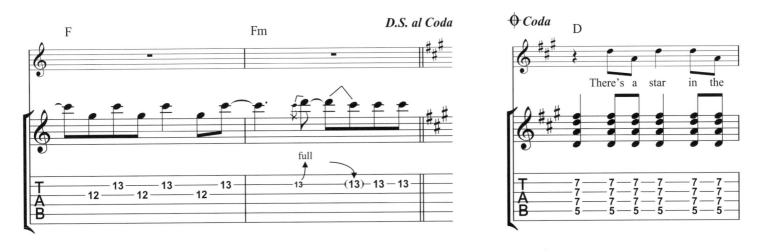

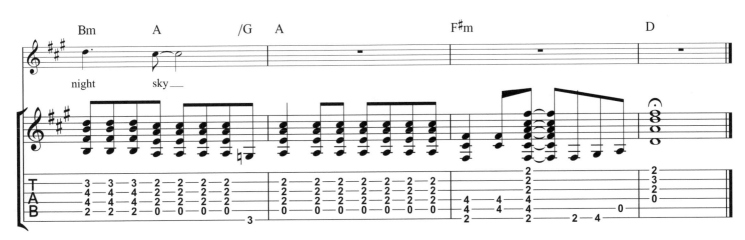

NUMBSKULL

WORDS BY TIM WHEELER
MUSIC BY MARK HAMILTON

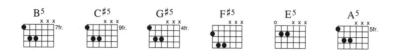

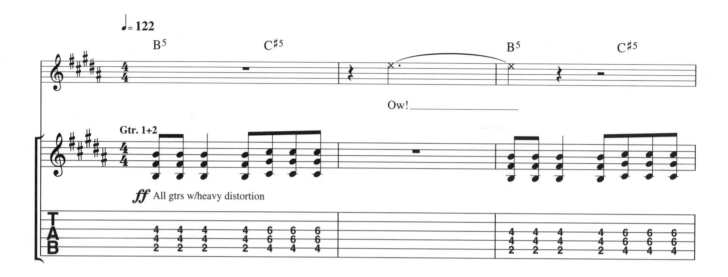

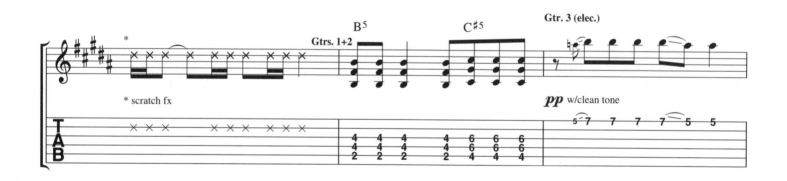

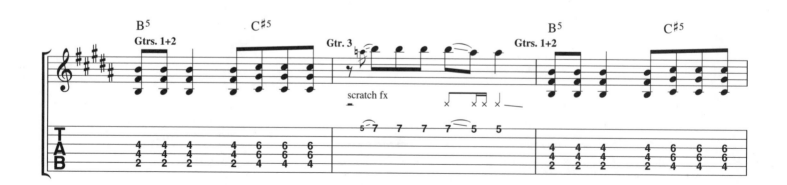

yeah death is your fate.___ __ Yeah death is your fate,___ come a - long for the ride.

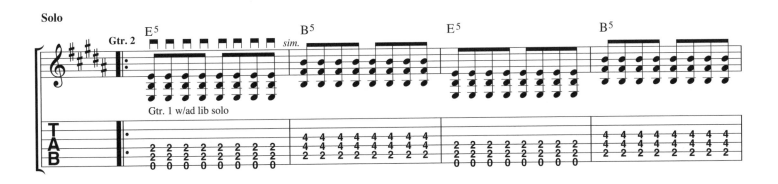

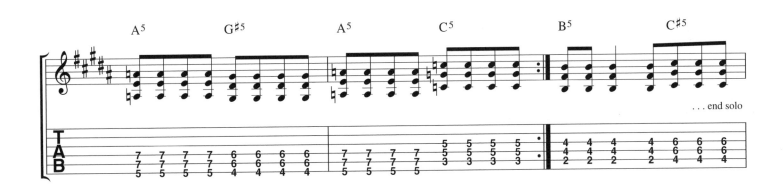

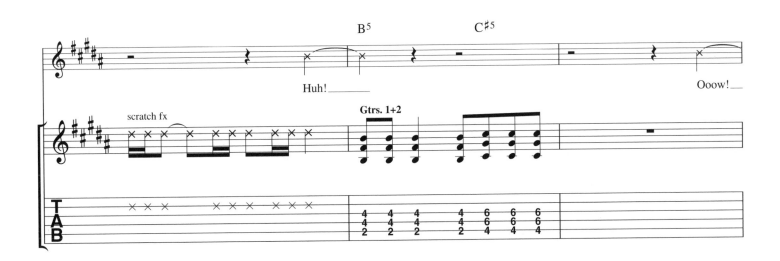

Huh!_____ Ooow!___

GUITAR TABLATURE EXPLAINED

Guitar music can be notated three different ways: on a musical stave, in tablature, and in rhythm slashes

RHYTHM SLASHES are written above the stave. Strum chords in the rhythm indicated. Round noteheads indicate single notes.

THE MUSICAL STAVE shows pitches and rhythms and is divided by lines into bars. Pitches are named after the first seven letters of the alphabet.

TABLATURE graphically represents the guitar fingerboard. Each horizontal line represents a string, and each number represents a fret.

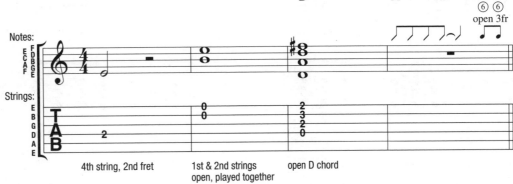

4th string, 2nd fret   1st & 2nd strings open, played together   open D chord

DEFINITIONS FOR SPECIAL GUITAR NOTATION

SEMI-TONE BEND: Strike the note and bend up a semi-tone (1/2 step).

WHOLE-TONE BEND: Strike the note and bend up a whole-tone (whole step).

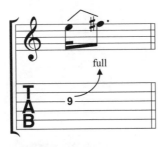

GRACE NOTE BEND: Strike the note and bend as indicated. Play the first note as quickly as possible.

QUARTER-TONE BEND: Strike the note and bend up a 1/4 step.

BEND & RELEASE: Strike the note and bend up as indicated, then release back to the original note.

COMPOUND BEND & RELEASE: Strike the note and bend up and down in the rhythm indicated.

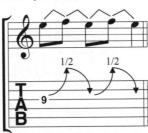

PRE-BEND: Bend the note as indicated, then strike it.

PRE-BEND & RELEASE: Bend the note as indicated. Strike it and release the note back to the original pitch.

HAMMER-ON: Strike the first note with one finger, then sound the second note (on the same string) with another finger by fretting it without picking.

PULL-OFF: Place both fingers on the notes to be sounded, strike the first note and without picking, pull the finger off to sound the second note.

LEGATO SLIDE (GLISS): Strike the first note and then slide the same fret-hand finger up or down to the second note. The second note is not struck.

MUFFLED STRINGS: A percussive sound is produced by laying the fret hand across the string(s) without depressing, and striking them with the pick hand.

NATURAL HARMONIC: Strike the note while the fret-hand lightly touches the string directly over the fret indicated.

PICK SCRAPE: The edge of the pick is rubbed down (or up) the string, producing a scratchy sound.

PALM MUTING: The note is partially muted by the pick hand lightly touching the string(s) just before the bridge.

SHIFT SLIDE (GLISS & RESTRIKE): Same as legato slide, except the second note is struck.

NOTE: The speed of any bend is indicated by the music notation and tempo.

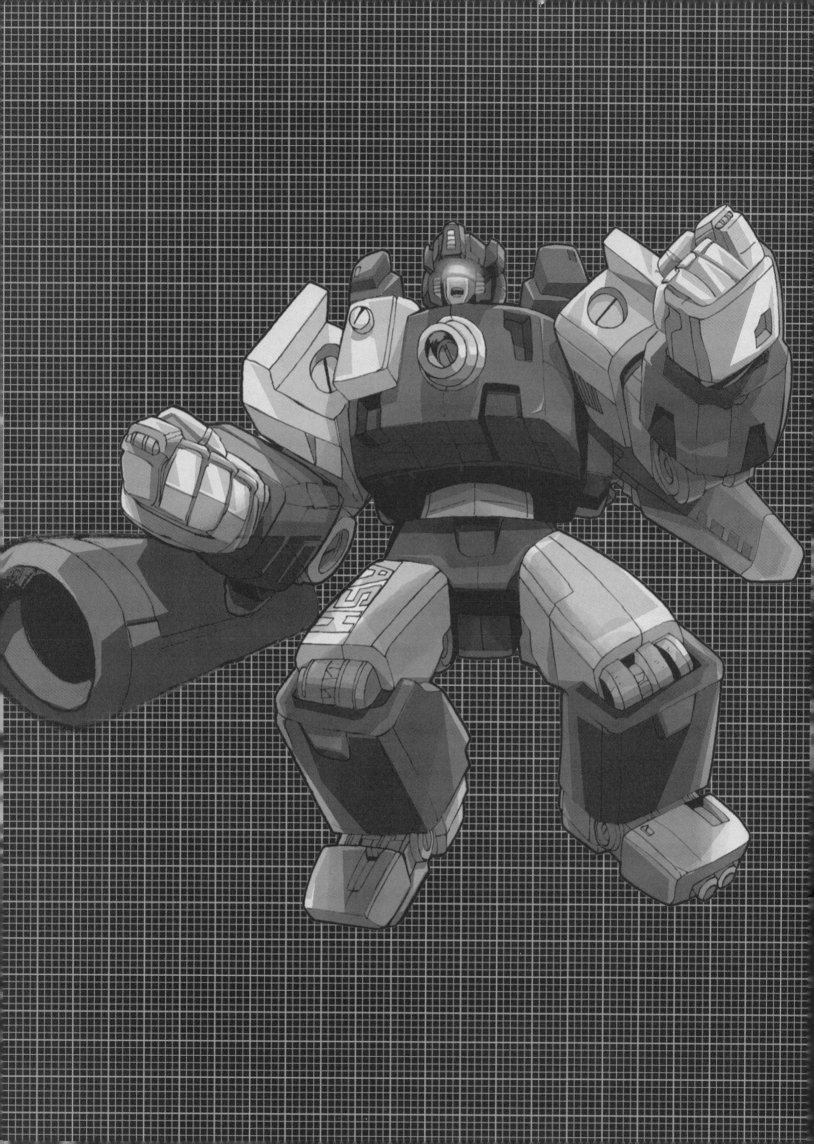